PUBLISHED FOR THE MALONE SOCIETY BY
OXFORD UNIVERSITY PRESS

GREAT CLARENDON STREET, OXFORD OX2 6DP

Oxford    New York
Auckland   Bangkok   Buenos Aires   Cape Town   Chennai
Dar es Salaam   Delhi   Hong Kong   Istanbul   Karachi   Kolkata
Kuala Lumpur   Madrid   Melbourne   Mexico City   Mumbai   Nairobi
São Paulo   Shanghai   Singapore   Taipei   Tokyo   Toronto

*British Library Cataloguing in Publication Data*
*A catalogue record for this book is available from the British Library*

*Library of Congress Cataloging in Publication Data*
*Data available*

ISBN 0 19 729044 2

*Printed by BAS Printers Limited, Salisbury, Wiltshire*

# COMMON CONDITIONS
## [?1576]

THE MALONE SOCIETY
REPRINTS, VOL. 168
2004

This edition of *Common Conditions* [?1576] was prepared by Roberta Barker, and checked by John Jowett, G. R. Proudfoot, and H. R. Woudhuysen.

The Society is grateful to the Elizabethan Club of Yale University, and especially to its Librarian, Stephen Parks, for permission to reproduce its unique copy of the book (EC 47).

*July 2004*          H. R. WOUDHUYSEN

# INTRODUCTION

*Common Conditions* was entered in the Register of the Stationers' Company on Thursday, 26 July 1576 to John Hunter, a Draper listed by Arber among those publishers not belonging to the Stationers' Company.[1] The entry is as follows:

> **Ihon hunter.** Receyued of him for his licence to ymprinte a newe and pleasant comedie or plaie after the man' of cõmon condycõns.              xij[d 2]

Two early quarto editions of the play survive, both in unique copies. The copy of the first quarto edition of the play (Q1), belonging to the Elizabethan Club at Yale University, is reproduced in this facsimile.[3] Its title-page states that it was 'Imprinted at London by Wil- | *liam How, for Iohn Hunter, dwel-* | lynge on London Birdge, at the | signe of the Blacke Lion', but bears no date of publication. The sole surviving copy of the second quarto of *Common Conditions* (Q2), which is in the Henry E. Huntington Library, is imperfect, wanting the first and last gatherings; its printer, publisher, and date are unknown.[4] Typographical evidence and extensive spelling and punctuation variants confirm that this fragmentary quarto represents a separate edition of the play, and that it is the later of the two editions.[5] If the Stationers' Register entry indicates the play's first publication, it seems reasonable to assume that How printed the quarto reproduced here for Hunter in 1576.

David Bevington has described *Common Conditions* as a typical product of English drama's transition from the traditional structures of the morality play to those of stage romance.[6] Named after its Vice figure (who is generally called 'Conditions', rather than 'Common Conditions', in the text proper), the play nevertheless 'substitut[es] a pilgrimage of adventure for a

---

[1] Edward Arber, *A Transcript of the Registers of the Company of Stationers of London*, 5 vols. (London and Birmingham, 1875–94), ii. 28.

[2] W. W. Greg, *A Bibliography of the English Printed Drama to the Restoration*, 4 vols. (London, 1939–59), i. 5; the entry transcribes Register B, fol. 134[r]. Edward Arber's transcription appears in *A Transcript of the Registers of the Company of Stationers of London*, ii. 301.

[3] Stephen Parks, *The Elizabethan Club of Yale University and Its Library* (New Haven, Conn., and London, 1986), p. 84.

[4] Greg, *Bibliography*, i. 149–51, nos. 69(*a*) and 69(*b*); STC 5592 and 5592a.

[5] Tucker Brooke, ed., *Common Conditions*, Elizabethan Club Reprints No. 1 (New Haven, Conn., and London, 1915), p. xii; see also Greg, *Bibliography*, i. 151.

[6] David M. Bevington, *From 'Mankind' to Marlowe: Growth of Structure in the Popular Drama of Tudor England* (Cambridge, Mass., 1962), p. 61.

pilgrimage of spiritual conflict'.[7] Its printed incarnation also conforms to Bevington's description of the bookselling practices of this transitional period. It appears to have been 'offered for acting': that is, intended for purchase by acting companies with an interest in playing it. Such works were habitually 'printed with casting lists to indicate how many actors are required to perform the play',[8] and indeed, the title-page of Q1 *Common Conditions* declares that 'Six may play this Comedie.' Bevington reads this statement as true,[9] but it may be a misrepresentation since the play's penultimate scene (TLN 1790–1850) involves as many as seven characters: Conditions, Lamphedon, Metrea (Clarisia), Lomia, Leostines, and 'a lorde or two more' (TLN 1790).[10] The permissive direction 'a lorde or two more' may indicate that the playwright was providing an opportunity for companies of six people to limit themselves to only one lord. Leostines, after all, addresses his companion(s) as 'My lorde' at TLN 1791. In TLN 1836, 'To waight on your honour, wee all are here prest', the line spoken by '*All.*' before they '*Exeunt.*', the 'wee' may include Lomia and Conditions and so accommodate the presence of only one Lord. The printed text could have been intended to offer flexible casting options for companies of different sizes. Nevertheless, the play's final scene (TLN 1851–1931) explicitly calls for 'two Lordes' (TLN 1851) in addition to Conditions, Lamphedon, Metrea/Clarisia, and Leostines. The actor playing Lomia is not needed in this scene, but any actor doubling her role with that of the second lord would have to change very rapidly indeed between lines 1837 and 1850. As Greg Walker has pointed out, 'Claims about the size of the cast needed to play a script were . . . occasionally no more than token assertions of their playability' in a competitive market where 'printers had to try all the tricks that they knew to increase the attractiveness of their products'.[11]

Whether or not *Common Conditions* was ever played by six actors, there remain indications, such as the dialogue from 'within' of the Mariners at TLN 1005–17, that the playwright wrote *Common Conditions* with doubling and its attendant costume changes in mind. The text also contains some striking features that may hint at its actual or intended theatrical life. The Prologue begins, 'You skilfull heads, that sit in place to see, likewise to

[7] Bevington, p. 193.
[8] Bevington, p. 5.
[9] Bevington, p. 72.
[10] In all quotations from the play its black-letter is represented by roman type and its roman type by italics; angled brackets are used to indicate incomplete speech prefixes and stage directions.
[11] Greg Walker, *The Politics of Performance in Early Renaissance Drama* (Cambridge, 1998), pp. 23–4.

heare, | What openly by Actours deeds in place shall straight appeare' (TLN 1–2) and draws to an end by asserting that 'the actours redy stand' (TLN 20). The language here suggests staging in the 'place' of a Tudor great hall, the performance site for which the vast majority of plays printed before 1580 were probably designed, with the actors standing ready to provide after-dinner entertainment for their noble employers.[12] By appealing to those that 'sit in place' the Prologue addresses the nobles seated at the dining table at the dais end of the hall and, more specifically, the educated spectators privileged to sit on benches on both sides of the playing 'place'.[13] The Prologue begs this educated audience not to despise the author's 'simple paine' (TLN 18), an appeal that conforms to Walker's description of much drama intended for great halls, in which 'the solemn supplications, the petitions and the statements of political import, seem clearly to have been directed squarely at the dais'.[14] Later in the play, Conditions appears to invoke a different contingent in the great hall audience when he demands 'Roome for a turne coate, that will turne as the wynde' (TLN 635) and 'rome for a cutter that is euery ynche a man' (TLN 928). Such addresses to the servants and other lower-class spectators standing around the screen end of the hall where the play was taking place are common in great hall plays, where 'the vices issued directly and noisily into and from the crowds of screens-enders voicing their arch variations of the popular "make room!" device'.[15] Moreover, Conditions first intervenes in the play by speaking from '*within*' (TLN 101), causing Sedmond to mistake him for 'an Ecco' (TLN 112). Such uses of offstage space were facilitated by the exits into kitchens and below-stairs apartments that stood at the screen end of many great halls, and would influence later staging practices in London's public theatres.

Although these references are typical of great hall drama, *Common Conditions* also contains other, less usual markers of a theatrical existence. For example, Conditions is described as 'litle' and 'littell' (TLN 257, 415) and as an 'elfe' (TLN 414, 1703), and must be small enough to climb a property tree at TLN 431, suggesting that the role may have been written with a boy actor in mind. More strikingly, at certain points the playtext specifies the imagined sources of its characters' entrances 'out of the wood' (TLN 302) and 'out of *Phrygia*' (TLN 488 and 521). Although the rapid shifts between localities that take place in *Common Conditions* are also noticeable in other plays of the period, such as *Clyomon and Clamydes* (?1570), these directions are exceptional. Chambers remarked that 'the episodes which follow these directions are not away from, but in the wood

[12] Walker, p. 34.  [13] See Walker, p. 53.  [14] Walker, p. 55.  [15] Walker, p. 57.

and Phrygia respectively; and the inference has been drawn that there were labelled doors, entrance through one of which warned the spectators that action was about to take place in the locality whose title the label bore'.[16] In support of this inference, Chambers cited Philip Sidney's *A Defence of Poetry*, where Sidney asked 'What Childe is there that, coming to a Play, and seeing *Thebes* written in great letters vpon an olde doore, doth beleeue that it is *Thebes*?' and complained of plays 'where you shal haue *Asia* of the one side, and *Affrick* of the other'.[17] However, as Chambers remarked, 'The whole business remains rather obscure.'[18] The stage directions in question may well have been intended as indications of location for the actors rather than as records of information relayed visually to the audience. Taken together with Sidney's comments, these directions support the notion that *Common Conditions* was intended for performance at the screen end of a great hall, with two potential entrance and exit points taken for granted.

Despite such traces of a theatrical existence, there is no solid evidence that *Common Conditions* was performed before its publication. Q1's title-page mentions neither an acting company nor a private group associated with it, nor any past performances. Moreover, the manuscript copy from which How set Q1 seems likely to have been authorial rather than theatrical, for the text of Q1 has features consistent with those of a draft. Speeches are wrongly assigned at TLN 593–6, 1197, 1468–72, 1560–4, and 1810. The stage direction '⟨Th⟩ey fight' appears at TLN 280 and '*Thei fig⟨ht⟩*' at TLN 1199, but a parallel direction is lacking for the duel between Lamphedon and Cardolus at 1355. Seven exits are missing (Conditions at TLN 748, Lamphedon and Clarisia at 998, Sabia at 1126, Cardolus and Lamphedon at 1381, Nomides at 1535, Conditions at 1619, and Leostines at 1683–4). The '*Exit*' at TLN 73 is misplaced, appearing to usher Clarisia offstage where the dialogue shows that it is in fact Galiarbus who exits two lines later (TLN 75). At TLN 709 Clarisia and Lamphedon are given the direction '*Exeunt*', but remain to speak with Conditions. However, some of these inconsistencies were probably caused by typographical considerations; for instance, Galiarbus' '*Exit*' is most likely relegated to TLN 73 because speech prefixes occupy the right margin for the following three lines, while Leostines' exit at TLN 1683–4 may be missing because it occurs after the last line of a very full page of type, followed by a line with a speech prefix in the right-hand margin. Moreover, loose or inconsistent use of entrances, exits, and stage

---

[16] E. K. Chambers, *The Elizabethan Stage*, 4 vols. (Oxford, 1923), iii. 40.
[17] Quoted in Chambers, iii. 40.
[18] Chambers, iii. 41.

directions is very common in printed playtexts of this period.[19] For example, on sig. A4[v] of *Appius and Virginia*, printed by How in 1575, the exit for Mater, Virginius, and Virginia is placed one line before they finish singing, while on sig. C3[r] the direction '*Here let Claudius go out with Haphazard.*' is followed three lines later by a marginal exit direction that clearly does not apply to Appius, who is speaking.[20] In the 1571 quarto of Richard Edwardes's *Damon and Pithias*, too, 'Exits are not so carefully marked [as entrances]' and are omitted in eight cases where 'the dialogue makes the action clear'.[21] Missing or misplaced stage directions or speech prefixes may, then, be a product of typographical considerations and need not be a sign of an authorial working draft.

The text contains a number of inconsistencies and other features that are vague or incompletely followed through. In one passage towards the end of the play Clarisia is referred to three times by her proper name rather than by Metrea, her disguised name: in dialogue at TLN 1837, in a stage direction at TLN 1852, and in a speech prefix at TLN 1886. This lapse may represent a moment in the author's draft, possibly written before the disguise name was chosen, and left unaltered. The tendency in the play's early scenes to designate the location from which the characters are entering ('out of the wood', TLN 302; 'out of *Phrygia*', TLN 488 and 521) disappears as the play progresses. Dialogue indicates that '*Lomia* the naturall,' (TLN 1411), carries a 'baby' (TLN 1426, 1446, 1526), perhaps a doll, but no stage directions indicate this. Most significantly, the play's plot appears obscure or incomplete at certain key points. Sir Nomides's speech at TLN 779–804 strongly implies that he is really Sedmond, but this is never confirmed. Many critics have guessed that Leostines is actually a disguised Galiarbus, but the text offers no definite support for this generically very reasonable hypothesis. Perhaps most indicative of all is the play's bizarre ending, in which Lamphedon and Clarisia/Metrea are apparently poisoned by Leostines, and the Epilogue declares that 'wee are now by Time cut of from farther time to spende' (TLN 1936), despite the fact that a number of the play's major plots remain unresolved. As Tucker Brooke noted, this conclusion is so sudden and surprising in relation to the rest of the play that readers aware only of the fragmentary second quarto have consistently

---

[19] See Linda McJannet, *The Voice of Elizabethan Stage Directions: The Evolution of a Theatrical Code* (Newark, NJ, and London, 1999), especially pp. 163–5.

[20] See Ronald B. McKerrow and W. W. Greg, eds., *Appius and Virginia 1575*, Malone Society Reprints (Oxford, 1911), TLN 201 (sig. A4[v]) and 638, 641 (sig. C3[r]).

[21] Arthur Brown and F. P. Wilson, eds., *Damon and Pythias*, Malone Society Reprints (Oxford, 1957), p. vii.

imagined a happy ending in its place.[22] Q1's abrupt ending might reflect a transcript of the play as abbreviated for the limited 'time' of the public stage. However, its conjunction with the text's other apparently incomplete or missing features may well suggest that the play text that has come down to us derives from the playwright's incompletely revised manuscript.

The identity of the author of *Common Conditions* has never been satisfactorily established. Fleay originally ascribed it to Robert Wilson, then rescinded 'that plausible hypothesis' and instead claimed the play for 'R. B. (Query Richard Bower), the author of *Appius and Virginia*' on the grounds that the style, metre, characterization, and use of alliteration in the two plays were highly similar.[23] In his edition of the play, Tucker Brooke dismissed Fleay's 'characteristic and unconvincing' argument.[24] He concurred, rather, with Greg's argument for an authorial link between *Common Conditions* and *Clyomon and Clamydes*, another transitional play, first printed in 1599, that combines the morality play's Vice figure with the plot conventions of romance. In his 1913 Malone Society edition of *Clyomon and Clamydes*, Greg noted Alexander Dyce's attribution of that play to George Peele. He remarked that although some critics have defended and many derided this attribution, 'no attempt has ever been made to show that the arguments advanced in support of this ascription would not equally prove Peele's authorship of *Common Conditions*, a very similar piece' to *Clyomon and Clamydes*.[25] Greg did not add that Peele, who was born in 1556, was very unlikely to have been the author of a play written about or even before the time he went up to Oxford in 1571. Glancing back to Fleay, Greg noted that Robert Wilson, Richard Bower, and Thomas Preston had also been proposed as the authors of *Clyomon and Clamydes* (and potentially, by extension, of *Common Conditions*), but that no convincing evidence supported such conjectures.[26] Tucker Brooke looked rather more favourably on Preston's claims to the play's authorship, arguing for its similarities with Preston's *Cambises*; however, he confessed that 'it would be decidedly hazardous to ascribe the work to him on the basis of our present knowledge'.[27] Drawing out the 'undoubtedly striking' links between *Common Conditions* and

---

[22] Tucker Brooke, ed., *Common Conditions*, p. xiii.

[23] Frederick Gard Fleay, *A Biographical Chronicle of the English Drama, 1559–1642*, 2 vols. (London, 1891), ii. 296.

[24] Tucker Brooke, *Common Conditions*, p. 83.

[25] W. W. Greg, ed., *Clyomon and Clamydes*, Malone Society Reprints (Oxford, 1913), pp. v–vi.

[26] Greg, *Clyomon*, p. vi.

[27] Tucker Brooke, *Common Conditions*, p. 84.

*Clyomon and Clamydes*, he nevertheless convincingly concluded that no authorship attribution should be attempted until 'we are more in a position than at present to estimate how far such devices belonged to the general repertory of dramatic writers at the time the plays were produced'.[28]

By 1926 Walter Harvey Worth answered Tucker Brooke's argument by suggesting that the similarities between *Common Conditions*, *Clyomon and Clamydes*, and other romances of the 1560s and 1570s were a result of court fashions in theatre. This made arguments for common authorship on the basis of similarity even less plausible, but equally it was based on the untested assumption that *Common Conditions* should be associated with the court.[29] In 1961, Jackson I. Cope revived the debate, arguing for the attribution of both *Common Conditions* and *Clyomon and Clamydes* to Richard Edwardes, Master of the Children of the Chapel Royal from 1561 to 1566 and author of *Damon and Pithias* (1565), on the grounds that the first two plays bear distinct similarities to the last.[30] However, Cope offered no convincing evidence for this proposition that could not equally be a sign of similarities between generically and historically congruent plays with different authors. His argument is further undermined by the fact that *Common Conditions* lacks several distinctive features of Edwardes's style, including the 'many Latin quotations' and the experimentation with rhyming patterns that Ros King notes in *Damon and Pithias*.[31] In 1913, Greg declared that 'All that can here be said is that *Clyomon and Clamydes* is very likely by the same hand as, and almost certainly contemporary with, *Common Conditions*'.[32] One hundred years later, even the attribution of the two plays to the same author remains a matter for debate, and the second half of Greg's declaration seems the more reliable.

The similarities between *Common Conditions* and *Clyomon and Clamydes* may, however, still provide the best clues as to the former's date of composition. The prayer for Queen Elizabeth that ends Q1 (TLN 1943–8) means that *Common Conditions* must date from after her accession to the

---

[28] Tucker Brooke, *Common Conditions*, p. 85. In *Defining Shakespeare: 'Pericles' as Test Case* (Oxford, 2003), p. 128, MacD. P. Jackson notes that the two plays share an unusually high number of instances when *the which* is not preceded by a preposition: eight times in *Common Conditions* and twenty-one times in *Clyomon and Clamydes*.

[29] Harvey Walter Worth, '*Damon and Pithias* and Related Plays', unpublished Ph.D. Dissertation (University of Chicago, 1926).

[30] Jackson I. Cope, '"The Best for Comedy": Richard Edwardes' Canon', *Texas Studies in Language and Literature*, 2 (1960–1), 501–19.

[31] Ros King, *The Works of Richard Edwards: Politics, Poetry and Performance in Sixteenth-Century England* (Manchester and New York, 2001), pp. 47, 52.

[32] Greg, *Clyomon*, p. vi.

throne in 1558; it was certainly in existence by 1576 when it was entered in the Stationers' Register. The play could have been written at any time between those dates, but it is usually dated to around 1576.[33] However, Q1 shows no evidence of the play's having been specially prepared for the press and gives no indication that it was composed in the period immediately preceding its entry in the Stationers' Register.

A reader convinced by Cope's argument in favour of Edwardes's authorship might be tempted to date the play's composition to the 1560s, close in time to *Damon and Pithias* and Edwardes's tenure in the Chapel Royal and before his death in 1566. However, since *Clyomon and Clamydes* remains the extant play most similar to *Common Conditions* in its language, prosody, dramatic conventions, and plot, it seems fair to assume with Greg that *Common Conditions* was composed around the same time as *Clyomon and Clamydes*. Greg argued that *Common Conditions* is probably later than *Clyomon and Clamydes*, but offered no evidence for the proposition.[34] Tucker Brooke believed, conversely, that *Common Conditions* is the earlier of the two plays on the grounds that the versification in *Clyomon and Clamydes* is 'distinctly more mature' than that in *Common Conditions*.[35] As this argument rests on an unsubstantiated assumption that the two plays share an author, it is probably best simply to suggest that *Common Conditions* was composed at about the same time as *Clyomon and Clamydes*, which dates from around 1570.[36]

The origins of *Common Conditions* are as obscure as its date and authorship. The title-page of Q1 states that the comedy is 'drawne out of the most famous historie of *Galiarbus* Duke of *Arabia*'. Considering the events of the play's plot, it seems reasonable to surmise that this 'famous historie' was a medieval or early modern prose romance, now lost; the *Short-Title Catalogue of Early English Books* has no likely match for such a romance, but it may have been a Continental rather than an English one. In 1904 Marie Gothein proposed an Italian play, Alessandro Piccolomini's *L'Amor Costante*, as a potential source for the play's main plot.[37] Her suggestion rested on the fact that both plays involve a banished father whose abandoned son and daughter are parted in their turn and, after numerous misadventures, meet again without recognizing one another. Other

[33] Alfred Harbage, *Annals of English Drama, 975–1700*, rev. S. Schoenbaum (Philadelphia, Pa., 1964), pp. 44–5.
[34] Greg, *Clyomon*, p. vi.
[35] Tucker Brooke, *Common Conditions*, p. 85.
[36] Harbage, *Annals of English Drama*, pp. 40–1; cf. Chambers, *Elizabethan Stage*, iv. 6.
[37] Marie Gothein, 'Die Frau im englischen Drama vor Shakespeare', *Shakespeare Jahrbuch*, 40 (1904), 1–50, at pp. 24–9.

similarities between the plays (for example, the love of a physician's daughter for the wandering son) are worth noting. However, Tucker Brooke convincingly contested Gothein's argument on the grounds that most of the parallels between the plays reflect narrative motifs common to many romances and are not strong enough to confirm a direct link between the two works.[38] That the play's major sources lie in the fruitful meeting between prose romance and the morality play tradition which also informs *Clyomon and Clamydes* is beyond question, but the particular romance that helped to shape the main plot and characters of *Common Conditions* remains unknown.

In terms of minor sources, Arbaccus, the name of the King of Arabia mentioned at TLN 26, recalls that given by Beaumont and Fletcher to Arbaces, King of Iberia in *A King and No King* (1619), and may possibly derive from Diodorus Siculus' description in the *Bibliotheca Historica* of a Median prince, Arbaces.[39] Ann Thompson has argued that the debate of Sabia and Nomides over the respective faithfulness of men and women in love (TLN 805–48) is borrowed from (or at least inspired by) Chaucer's *Legend of Good Women*, and that the author's use of this source reflects his recognition of Chaucerian irony.[40] Sabia uses Dido, Medea, and Ariadne, all heroines of the *Legend*, as examples supporting her argument in favour of women's faithfulness; the fact that she names them and their stories in the same order as Chaucer may indeed suggest that the author of *Common Conditions* was thinking of the *Legend* here. Sabia's mockery of Nomides' use of 'auctors' as an aid in disputation (TLN 828–9) also recalls Chaucerian language and themes, while Nomides's condemnation of Cressida (TLN 820) may hint at some awareness of *Troilus and Criseyde*. Sabia's riposte, with its description of Cressida as 'like Lazer faine to sit and beg' (TLN 842), probably alludes to Robert Henryson's *The Testament of Cresseid* or to the large ballad literature that had accrued to the Cressida legend by the time *Common Conditions* was written. As most of the references to faithless and faithful women in the Sabia–Nomides debate similarly recall stories common to many early modern sources, it is difficult to prove that Chaucer was the playwright's direct source for this passage. Like the classical authors—Seneca, Ovid, Cicero, and Homer—cited admiringly in the Prologue to *Common Conditions*, Chaucer may perhaps best be regarded as a general influence rather than a specific source.

[38] C. F. Tucker Brooke, 'On the Sources of Common Conditions', *Modern Language Notes*, 31 (1916), 474–8.

[39] See Francis Beaumont and John Fletcher, *A King and No King*, ed. Robert K. Turner, Jr. (London, 1964), p. xiv.

[40] R. Ann Thompson, 'The Irony of Chaucer's *Legend of Good Women* Perceived in 1576', *Archiv*, 213 (1976), 342–3.

The name of John Hunter, the publisher of the first quarto of *Common Conditions*, occurs in only one other book, *The ruinate fall of the pope Vsury, deriued from the pope Idolatrie, reueled by a Saxon antiquitie*. This dialogue between flesh and spirit was printed by John Allde in about 1580 and survives in a unique copy in the Huntington Library: Hunter's address in this book places his shop on London Bridge, as does *Common Conditions*.[41] The play's printer, William How, is known to have worked in London from 1565 until about 1591: on the surviving evidence his most active years were 1569–70 and 1575. He printed a fairly wide variety of material, including several volumes of poetry. He had printed three plays before *Common Conditions*: William Wager's *The Longer thou Livest the More Fool thou Art* of about 1569, *New Custom* (1573), and R.B.'s *Appius and Virginia* (1575).[42] These show some typographic similarities with *Common Conditions*, but there are also significant differences: for example, the beginning of each speech in *New Custom* is generally signalled with a pilcrow and speech prefixes in *Appius and Virginia* are centred in roman type, whereas in *Common Conditions* the first lines of speeches are indented and speech prefixes are set in the outer margin.

Q1 *Common Conditions*, which consists of twenty-eight unnumbered leaves, collates A–G⁴. There are no act or scene divisions, but new scenes generally begin with pilcrows preceding stage directions for entries. Q1 is largely printed in black letter (20 lines = 82 mm), with roman type for incidental use, especially for proper names (including speech prefixes). The first of the play's two songs (TLN 217–48) is printed mostly in a larger black-letter fount; the second (TLN 1153–74) is printed wholly in the same larger fount.[43] A smaller black-letter fount occurs in lines 7 and 8 of the title-page and in the marginal stage direction in TLN 159. Entrance directions are generally centred, set in black letter, and always preceded by a pilcrow. The centred direction at TLN 1005 is a stage direction for the first offstage utterances of the Mariners and the Epilogue is announced at TLN 1932 with a centred heading in roman type. The entrance signalled at TLN 1691–2 is set in the outer margin. Other directions usually appear either in roman, or occasionally, in black letter, on the right within the measure.[44] Speech

[41] STC 24557.5.
[42] Greg, *Bibliography*, nos. 53(*A*), 59(*A*), 65(*A*). The songs in *Appius and Virginia* (B2ᵛ–3ʳ) are set in the same larger type as the songs in *Common Conditions*.
[43] The larger fount also occurs in lines 3 and 27 of the play's title-page.
[44] See TLN 73, 101, 214, 431, 435, 458, 622, 637, 709, 739, 903, 912, 1073, 1112, 1222, 1278, 1303, 1524, 1527, 1612, 1765, 1836. A few directions are set (almost all in roman) in the outer margin among the speech prefixes; see TLN 75, 159 (black letter), 217–18, 280, 301–2, 1199, 1691–2 (black letter and roman).

prefixes appear in roman in the outer margin, and are frequently affected by the cropping of the edges of the Elizabethan Club copy. The first line of speeches is generally indented.[45] After entrances the first line of the following speech usually begins with a two-line roman drop-capital.[46] There is one line of continuous printing on B3$^v$ where Conditions and Drift both have speeches in the same line (TLN 419).

The quarto's title-page is decorated with ornaments forming a single lace border which appears in a double form on the title-page of How's printing of *Appius and Virginia*. The title-page is sig. A1$^r$; sig. A1$^v$ is blank; the text begins on A2$^r$ and ends on G4$^v$ with 'FINIS.' and a printer's ornament. The first three leaves of each gathering are signed with lower-case roman numerals, except for A1$^r$ and B3$^r$, which are unsigned. Most pages have a depth of 37 lines (including blank lines) or, as on the pages with larger type (A4$^v$–B1$^r$, E1$^v$–E2$^r$), the equivalent. However, there are only 36 lines on G4$^r$, and 38 lines on pages B1$^v$, B3$^r$, C4$^r$, F1$^v$, F4$^r$, and G3$^v$. Catchwords generally appear in the direction line, but they are missing on all the 38-line pages and on C3$^v$. Spacing around stage directions is variable.[47]

The fact that all the 38-line pages (with the exception of B3$^r$) occur in the inner forme can be associated with the relatively loose setting of several pages: D2$^r$, D3$^v$, E1$^v$, E2$^r$, G1$^v$, G3$^r$, G4$^r$, and G4$^v$. With the exception of some pages in G these are all inner-forme pages; since they are in the perfecting forme their looseness, if it signifies anything, may be a sign of adjustment of copy on pages where space remains to be filled. The irregularities in G may be accounted for by its being the last gathering, and by a wish to leave enough copy for its final page.

These variations in page length and lineation might be taken as a sign that Q1 was cast off for setting by formes. An analysis of the book's headlines offers further evidence that this was the case. Headlines are consistent from A2$^v$ to C3$^r$, suggesting the use of one skeleton forme: the only exception is A4$^v$, whose headline ends in a full stop rather than the usual comma. This headline was corrected to a comma when it was used again on A3$^v$; the fact

[45] There are exceptions at TLN 422, 435, 716, 779, 990, 1112, 1357, 1758, where the measure of the line is full. The compositor sometimes failed to indent the first line of speeches when they began a new page, as at TLN 110, 1757, 1794, and made errors in relation to indentation at TLN 593 and 597, 1197–8, 1562–3, 1738–9.

[46] This does not occur in TLN 121, 217, 660, 779, 1006, 1019, 1153, 1691, 1902; however, similar capitals are used to signal the start of the song at TLN 219 following the two songs at TLN, 249, 1175.

[47] Blank lines are left before and after the stage directions or headings on A2$^r$, G4$^r$; there is a blank line before the directions on D2$^r$, G1$^r$, G3$^r$; shallower blank lines are left around the direction on A4$^v$ (before the first song), on B4$^v$, and around the two directions on D3$^v$.

that such an anomaly occurs in the outer forme of A suggests that this forme may have been printed first. Other evidence from headlines supports this hypothesis. In the headline of C4$^v$, a flaw appears in the type of the terminal comma; this flaw is visible on C3$^v$ and on pages 3$^v$ in the inner forme and 4$^v$ in the outer forme for all gatherings thereafter. On E1$^r$ 'condicions' becomes 'condicion', perhaps as a result of the accidental loss of the last letter. This version of the headline continues to appear on pages 1$^r$ on the outer forme and 2$^r$ on the inner forme for all gatherings thereafter.

There is not sufficient evidence for any conclusions to be drawn from type shortages, which are not very great and which, because of the trimming of margins which affected speech prefixes, cannot all be recovered. There are shortages in all formes except for inner A and both formes of B.[48]

Q1 makes frequent use of abbreviations, such as 'y$^t$' for 'that', 'y$^u$' for 'thou', 'y$^e$' for 'the', and 'w$^t$' for 'with'. It often uses the tilde to replace a missing 'n,' as in 'Conditiõs', and an ampersand for 'and'. These abbreviations are usually employed to save space (see, for example, the long line at TLN 1476, which uses four abbreviations), and often appear on the same page as the unabbreviated form of the same word. Analysis of Q1's spellings offers no conclusive evidence for the presence of more than one compositor. Some frequently used words, such as 'knight' and the oath 'gogs bloud', appear consistently in one form. Other common words, however, appear in many variant spellings. For example, the word 'soil' (a favourite of the play's author) appears at TLN 24 and 97 as 'soyll' and as 'soile' (TLN 151) before taking its most common spelling, 'soyle' (for instance, at TLN 304, 325, 780, 951, 1340, 1695). In addition to the unusual spelling of 'soyll' on sig. A2$^r$ the form 'Syer' occurs in the same line (TLN 24) for a word that thereafter appears in Q1 as 'Sier' or 'sier' (for instance, at TLN 42, 975, 1099, 1103, 1635), or occasionally 'sire' (TLN 147). Such evidence is not sufficient to suggest a change of compositors, however, as A2$^r$ also contains a number of spellings that recur throughout the quarto, such as 'Sutch' for 'Such' (TLN 28). The spelling of this last word frequently varies in Q1, appearing usually as 'sutch', but also as 'such' (TLN 150, 581, 894, 895, 1818), 'suche' (TLN 1000, 1572), and 'sutche' (TLN 1015) on sig. D3$^v$, which also has 'suche' (TLN 1000). Single pages frequently use multiple spellings of the same word: for instance, 'king' and 'kinge' (TLN 512, 517)

[48] The substitutions replace an upper-case roman C with a lower-case one, an upper-case black-letter W with a lower-case one or with a swash one, and an upper-case roman L with a small capital one or (once) with an upper-case italic one. A roman for an italic A on A1$^r$ line 4 may simply be an error.

appear on C1$^r$, 'weemen' and 'wemen' on sig. D1$^r$ (TLN 810, 811, 815), and 'captayne', 'Captayne', and 'Captaine' on sig. D4$^r$ (TLN 1055, 1057, 1060). The forms of speech prefixes also vary a great deal, with the title character's name appearing on sig. B3$^v$ alone as '*Condiciõs*', '*Conditiõs*', '*Cõditions*', '*Conditiõs.*', '*Condit.*', and '*Condi.*' (TLN 400, 403, 411, 420, 424, 431). Even the less variant '*Clarisia.*' appears on sig. E3$^r$ as both '*cla.*' and '*Clarisia*' (TLN 1242, 1248) without obvious typographical reasons for the variation. Thus, although a page like A4$^r$ may stand out as containing a number of rare or unique spellings (including the quarto's only use of the symbol ꝗ for 'quoth' at TLN 161), the frequency of different spelling forms throughout the quarto precludes any attempt at making compositor identification certain. It is only to be expected that variations in different forms of words occur towards the beginning of the process of setting type before the compositor has decided which forms to use.

The surviving copy of the second quarto of *Common Conditions* consists of only twenty unnumbered leaves. In addition to its missing title-page, it lacks all leaves before B1 and after F4; B1 is extensively damaged. As Greg noted, the type of Q2 *Common Conditions* is different from that of Q1, as are the running titles.[49] The page-division and typographical arrangement of the two editions also differ. On B1$^r$, the first surviving page of Q2, the second line of the song (TLN 220) has been divided into two lines, the second consisting of the equivalent of 'our mirth shall augment': this was probably caused by the use in Q2 of a large, three-line drop capital. Q2's text moves on to the next page one line behind Q1's from B1$^v$ to B3$^r$, but the last two lines on that page in Q1 (TLN 397–8) are moved from there in Q2 to begin B3$^v$; its text begins B4$^r$ two behind Q1's, but finishes the page one line behind Q1 by moving the stage direction in TLN 458 into the preceding line. B4$^v$ in Q2 therefore begins one line behind Q1 but finishes in the same place by removing space around the stage direction in TLN 488. The page-division of the two editions is identical from C1$^r$ to C3$^v$; on the foot of C4$^r$ Q2 falls one behind Q1 and continues in this way until D2$^r$ where the line is made up by removing the space before the stage direction in Q1's TLN 913. From D2$^v$ to F1$^r$ the page-division of the two editions is again equivalent; on F1$^v$ Q2's text again falls one line behind Q1's, probably because the turn up necessary to complete the equivalent of Q1's TLN 146 ('(a knife' in Q2) would not fit into Q2's TLN 1459, which was made longer by the presence of a three-line drop capital letter beginning TLN 1457. Q2 remains one line behind Q1 from F2$^r$ to F4$^r$ where it falls two lines behind, a state maintained on F4$^v$, the final extant page of Q2. In other words, as Tucker Brooke notes, seventeen

---

[49] Greg, *Bibliography*, i. 150.

of the forty pages shared by the two quartos end at different lines.[50] The drop-capitals in Q2 are generally larger and more elaborate than those in Q1. Q2 frequently normalized Q1's abbreviations, typically using 'the' for Q1's 'y$^e$' and 'that' for Q1's 'y$^t$'. Q2 often, although not always, used 'and' where Q1 has an ampersand. These changes may indicate that space-saving was less of a problem for Q2's compositor than for Q1's. On the other hand, Q2 regularly used the symbol ꝙ for the word 'quoth' (as already noted, this symbol only appears once in Q1, at TLN 161). The compositor of Q2 preferred to use 'ie' at the end of words that Q1's compositor usually spelled with a 'y'. Commas appear much more frequently in Q2 than in Q1. These last two forms of variance can be seen clearly in a comparison between the first three lines on sig. B2$^r$ (the first page of Q2 which survives in full) and the equivalent lines in Q1 (TLN 286–8). Q1 reads, 'The Gentelman with his lady intend to come this way, | And therfore let vs be all in one minde, and agre all together, | For I know it will not be long or they come hether.' Q2 reads, 'The gentleman with his Ladie, intende to come this waie. | And therefore let vs bee all in one minde, and agree all together, | For I knowe it will not bee long, or thei come hether.' Such differences of spelling and punctuation recur throughout Q1 and Q2 and may suggest that different compositors set the two editions.

The collation of substantive variants that follows shows Q2 sometimes correcting apparently erroneous readings in Q1 and sometimes introducing what appear to be fresh errors in place of Q1's probably correct readings. The two editions share a number of doubtful readings, such as the conspicuous 'aged' in place of 'a god' to describe Cupid at Q1 TLN 897. Tucker Brooke convincingly argued that these points suggest that Q1 served as the printer's copy for Q2.[51] However, the fact (unmentioned by Tucker Brooke) that both misassign speeches at TLN 1468–72 and at 1560–4, but make different errors in doing so, might also suggest that both compositors were using the same manuscript of the play as a copy-text and that the manuscript was unclear at these points. It may, however, seem more likely that the errors here represent a failed attempt by the compositor of Q2 to rectify the misassigned speeches in Q1.

Although the appeal of *Common Conditions* prompted these two separate editions in its own time, it seems rapidly to have become a rarity both in performance and in print. The play is mentioned in Rogers and Ley's and Archer's catalogues of 1656 as 'Common conditions, C[omedy]'. It appears

---

[50] Tucker Brooke, *Common Conditions*, pp. xi–xii.
[51] Tucker Brooke, *Common Conditions*, p. xii.

in both the 1661 and 1671 editions of Francis Kirkman's Catalogue of Plays as 'Comons conditions'.[52] In his *Account of the English dramatick poets*, Gerard Langbaine was probably working from Kirkman's lists when he described the play as '*Commons Condition*, a Comedy which I never saw'.[53] In *The lives and characters of the English dramatick poets* (1699), Langbaine tried to make better sense of the earlier erroneous title of the play and further remarked on '*The Commons Condition*, a Comedy, of which I can give no Account'.[54] This may suggest that by 1699 printed copies of the play had become difficult to find. A century later a copy of the play was available to Isaac Reed for his supplement of 'Additions and Corrections' to the second volume of David Baker's *Biographia Dramatica* (1782). Reed corrected Baker's listing of the title as *The Common's Condition*, and described the play as 'to all appearance as ancient as *Gammer Gurton*', and containing 'perhaps the earliest examples of naval dialogue on the stage, as well as of the English language distorted by foreign pronunciation'. Reed's source was the unique surviving imperfect copy of Q2, for he noted that 'the copy before me wants both the first and concluding leaves'.[55] This same copy was transcribed for Edmond Malone while it was in the possession of Dr Richard Wright of Charles Street, Grosvenor Square, London.[56] George Steevens bought the book in 1787; it passed from him to the Duke of Roxburghe (1800), from thence to Richard Heber (1812), and finally to the Duke of Devonshire (1834). It was kept in the library at Chatsworth House until 1914, when it was sold to Henry Huntington.[57] The imperfect copy of this edition remained the only available source for critics of the play until 1907, when the London bookdealer Bernard Quaritch bought the copy of Q1 reproduced here at a sale of books from the library of Lord Mostyn.[58] On the evidence of

[52] Greg, *Bibliography*, iii. 1322, 1331, 1342.

[53] Gerard Langbaine, *An account of the English dramatick poets* (London, 1691), p. 528.

[54] Gerard Langbaine, *The lives and characters of the English dramatick poets* (London, 1699), p. 158.

[55] David Erskine Baker, *Biographia Dramatica, or, A Companion to the Playhouse*, 2nd edn. supplemented by Isaac Reed, 2 vols. (London, 1782), ii. 436–7.

[56] Tucker Brooke, *Common Conditions*, p. xi. In *Five Anonymous Plays (Fourth Series)*, ed. John S. Farmer, for the Early English Drama Society (London, 1908), p. 181, Farmer noted the existence of a transcript made by Malone in the Bodleian Library, Oxford. In fact the transcript, in two different hands, was made for Malone and is in MS Malone 32, fols. 87$^r$–109$^v$; another copy made from Malone's transcript is in the Dyce Collection of the National Art Library at the Victoria and Albert Museum (Dyce MS 15) and is on paper watermarked 1827. An earlier transcript made by John Henderson of the Covent Garden Theatre was lot 648 in the sale of his books on 20 Feb. 1786 and fetched £1. 18s.

[57] See Tucker Brooke, *Common Conditions*, p. xi.

[58] It was lot 437 in Sotheby's sale of 1 June 1907 and given to Yale by Alexander S. Cochran in Dec. 1911.

Lord Mostyn, Tucker Brooke suggested that Q1 entered the library at Mostyn Hall, North Wales, in about 1690, along with copies of John Heywood's *The Four P's* and John Phillip's *Patient and Meek Grissell*, which were cropped almost identically.[59] Along with these two quartos, the Elizabethan Club Library, Yale University, now owns Q1 *Common Conditions*. Q2 was reprinted in 1898 by Alois Brandl and in 1908 by John S. Farmer.[60] The only previously edited text of Q1 is that of Tucker Brooke.

Tucker Brooke's edition includes a brief discussion of one special characteristic of the Elizabethan Club's copy of Q1 of interest to students of the play. It contains a number of interlinear notes in one or more sixteenth-century hands, which are transcribed at the end of this Introduction. On C1$^r$, Lamphedon's speech has been annotated in black ink and secretary hand at TLN 524–39. On C2$^v$ Clarisia's speech has been annotated extensively in black ink and in secretary hand between TLN 638 and 656. Some of these notes are quite lengthy and are copied into the margins of the volume, in three cases adding new sets of rhyming couplets to the printed text. On C4$^r$ brief annotations in brown ink and in secretary hand have been made to Sabia's soliloquy at TLN 754, 757, and 758, with very faint annotations also visible at 766 and 768. Similarly brief annotations have also been made to the same speech on C4$^v$ at TLN 770–1. On D2$^r$, Sabia's speech has been annotated in brown ink and in secretary hand at TLN 904–9. All of these speeches concern the vagaries of love. The earlier ones have been revised by the annotator to reflect a poor lover's plea to a maiden of 'suffolke' variously referred to as 'sweet Anne' and 'Agnis'; at TLN 532 and 655 he replaces the names of the speakers with 'Amos', perhaps his own Christian name or a romantic pseudonym. The relationship between the suffolk lovers caused the annotator to reverse the gender and status of characters in *Common Conditions* to suit his or her purpose. Sabia's speeches have been revised to reflect the love of a lady for 'Edward Dear'. Tucker Brooke assumed that these annotations express 'the love of the owner of the book'.[61] It is also possible that they represent a more general exercise in the creation of love poetry, a dialogue between two lovers (real or imaginary), or even a revision of these speeches for use in a new play or entertainment—one that presumably would exclude the rest of the material from *Common Conditions*.

[59] Tucker Brooke, *Common Conditions*, p. x; when Quaritch bought the three plays they were disbound.

[60] Alois Brandl, *Quellen des weltlichen Dramas in England vor Shakespeare*, Quellen und Forschungen zur Sprach- und Culturgeschichte der germanischen Völker, 80 (1898). Farmer's edition of *Five Anonymous Plays (Fourth Series)* was reprinted in facsimile in 1966 by Charles W. Traylen (Guildford).

[61] Tucker Brooke, *Common Conditions*, p. 87.

Some Elizabethan inhabitants of Suffolk, the county referred to by the annotator, collected playbooks for use in the organizing and staging of theatricals. For instance, at his death in 1595 Bennett Kynge, a surgeon of Bungay, owned a box of 'play boockes' and another of 'dysgysings for players'.[62] The personal 'borrowing' of quotations from printed works is familiar from many early modern manuscript miscellanies and letter-books. Unless the identity of Q1's annotator can be established, the status and significance of these interlineations must remain uncertain.

Further questions are raised by a final, striking annotation in mixed italic and secretary hand, added below the printer's ornament on the final page of this copy. It seems to be of the same period as the earlier annotations and may be in the same hand. The writer began in Latin: '*Etsi (m.p.) hæc fabula*', then stopped, repeated the bracketed initials, and started a new annotation in Latin and Greek. This annotation reads as follows: '*Etsi est ἔωλος hæc fabula præsertim tantis novis rebus: tamen perire meam lucubrationem nolui*'. This may be translated as, 'Even though this story is stale, especially after such new things [or events]: yet I do not wish my midnight labours to perish.' As Tucker Brooke noted, the annotator was here recalling Cicero's *Epistolae ad Familiares*, IX.2.1: '*etsi erat ἔωλος illa epistula, praesertim tantis postea novis rebus adlatis, tamen perire lucubrationem meam nolui.*'[63] If we see the annotator's use of *lucubrationem*, 'midnight labours', as applying to the play as a whole, we may be tempted to imagine the author himself looking back on its writing—and perhaps even at an earlier attempt at revision. Although this hypothesis is enticing, the play itself offers no evidence that its author was given to quoting (or, as in this case, misquoting) Latin authors. It seems more plausible to see this as the hand of the book's earlier annotator, looking back on his follies and 'labours' as a young lover. Regardless of the annotator's identity and motives, his reference to Cicero is revealing and offers us a brief glimpse of an early modern reaction to the passing of the transitional form of drama represented by *Common Conditions*.

\*

I should like to thank Dr Martin Wiggins and the students of the Shakespeare Institute, Stratford-upon-Avon, for their observations on *Common Conditions*, which have contributed greatly to this Introduction.

[62] David Dyamond, 'Three Entertainers from Tudor Suffolk', *Records of Early English Drama Newsletter*, 16.1 (1991), 2–5, at p. 2.
[63] Cicero, *Epistulae ad Familiares*, ed. D. R. Shackleton Bailey, 2 vols. (Cambridge, 1977), ii. 7 (no. 177.9–11).

# ERRONEOUS AND DOUBTFUL READINGS IN Q1

This list does not duplicate the following collation of substantive variants between Q1 and Q2. The brackets contain possible corrected readings, with their sources, where relevant. In his edition of the play Tucker Brook records the emendations in the Dyce MS and conjectured (privately) by John M. Manly.

| | |
|---|---|
| Title-page line 27 | Birdge (*Bridge*) |
| 13 | exeeede (*exceed*) |
| 303 | vs (*is*) |
| 362 | mastery (*e* damaged) |
| 453 | Whom (*who* Tucker Brooke conj.) |
| 472 | did I not (*did I* Tucker Brooke suggests an error caused by the following line) |
| 514 | atacht (*atache* Tucker Brooke) |
| 525 | thee (*tree*) |
| 593–6 | Each of the speech prefixes for these lines is placed one line too low |
| 682 | Knight (*t* damaged) |
| 700 | Lacks speech prefix for Clarisia |
| 852 | by their (*by your* Tucker Brooke) |
| 897 | aged (*a god* Dyce MS) |
| 1151 | deride (*devide* Manly conj.) |
| 1178 | Desirous (*Desire us* Tucker Brooke) |
| 1197 | Speech prefix set one line too high |
| 1315 | Beehold (*Bee bold* Tucker Brooke) |
| 1361 | it (*yet* Tucker Brooke) |
| 1392 | Whom (*Who* Tucker Brooke) |
| 1470 | Lacks speech prefix, probably for Nomides |
| 1563 | Speech prefix should be set at 1562. Q2 provides the speech prefix 'Condi' for TLN 1561. It then assigns TLN 1562–3 to Conditions before assigning TLN 1564 to Lamphedon. From the context, it seems clear that both quartos are incorrect. TLN 1560–1 should be assigned to Conditions and TLN 1562–6 to Lamphedon. |
| 1731 | Bee (*By*) |
| 1810 | *Lomia.* (*Lords*) |

xxii

| 1823 | loue (*true*) |
| 1841 | diseases (*disease*) |
| 1859 | dist (*didst*) |
| 1860 | Is thy (*Is this thy*) |
| 1875 | sust ine (*sustaine*) |
| 1882 | srught (*sought*) |
| 1946 | eares (*yeares*) |

# SUBSTANTIVE VARIANTS BETWEEN Q1 (ELIZABETHAN CLUB) AND Q2 (HUNTINGTON LIBRARY)

This collation begins on B1ʳ, the first extant page of Q2 *Common Conditions*. B1 is badly damaged; the first undamaged page of Q2 *Common Conditions* is B2ʳ. Q2 ends on E4ᵛ at Q1's TLN 1681. Its final catchword, 'No,' shows a substantive variant with TLN 1682 of Q1. In the following list the quarto's black-letter type has been rendered as roman and its roman as italic.

| *Line number in Q1* | *Q1* | *Q2* |
|---|---|---|
| 260 | his quoine | this coigne |
| 309 | good sister be of chere | sister bee of good chere |
| 324 | to foraine | in foraine |
| 349 | bee | hee [?damaged] |
| 359 | vnto ire | to ire |
| 373 | their company? | your companie? |
| 378 | and end | an ende |
| 389 | you are fast now | your are faste, |
| 393 | Ah | Oh |
| 418 | now | not |
| 435 | ⟨A⟩mob. | *Ambo.* |
| 474 | gods | God |
| 526 | a cause | the cause |
| 534 | Duke of *Phrygia* noble soyle | Duke, of *Pririgia* noble soile |
| 574 | beseeke | beseche |
| 590 | waies | waie |
| 609 | here in | herein |
| 618 | for to beare | to beare |
| 628 | thereis a nother | there is an other |
| 658 | as louer still | a louer still |
| 682 | Knighc | knight |
| 735 | redy am to waight | readie am on you to waight |
| 758 | doth the flower | doeth the flowers |
| 796 | murdering | murtheryng |
| 808 | meuer | neuer |
| 826 | neclect | neglect |
| 843 | to men | in men |

| | | |
|---|---|---|
| 844 | for go | forgo |
| 852 | Yee | Yea |
| 855 | witles | witnesse |
| 871 | Na | Naie |
| 875 | thesame | the same |
| 878 | flight | slight |
| 892 | tobreede | to breede |
| 914 | geare cottens | greare cottes |
| 924 | to vnkle | an vnkle |
| 926 | at the | the |
| 943 | in continent | incontinent |
| 948 | Wheras | Whereas |
| 956 | $^{I}$you | ye yet |
| 1003 | *Thracie* | *Tharcie* |
| 1010 | *Lamphe* & *Cla.* | *Lãphedõ* & *Clarisia* |
| 1015 | cannot | can not |
| 1042 | Because | Be cause |
| 1061 | you | ye |
| 1067 | a boundance | aboundance |
| 1078 | a frayda | afraida |
| 1083 | cannot | can not |
| 1086 | yee | be |
| 1093 | Gentelmana, or knighta, | Gentelman, or knighte, |
| 1099 | you | ye |
| 1105 | *Monuta* | Mount [s.p.] |
| 1148 | for got | forgot |
| 1198 | They were | Thei are |
| 1200 | hereof | here of |
| 1207 | Thy | The |
| 1225 | liue a | liue in |
| 1228 | for to subdew | to subdue |
| 1230 | the | thee |
| 1232 | *Herculus* | *Hercules* |
| 1235 | berife | be rife |
| 1250 | be come | become |
| 1265 | but | not but |
| 1277 | M. & my good Ms. | master & my good mist. |
| 1279 | vs haue | vs to haue |
| 1293 | ill | ile |
| 1314 | deuice | deuide |

| | | |
|---|---|---|
| 1317 | sammon | summon |
| 1339 | prepare, to try | prepare to |
| 1345 | the victory | victorie |
| 1367 | All though | Although |
| 1374 | the | thy |
| 1389 | orforce | or force |
| 1401 | dispayre | to dispaire |
| 1424 | My Lady wilbe | And my Ladie will be |
| 1435 | go play. | plaie, |
| 1443 | wilbe | will be |
| 1447 | mocke | mocke me |
| 1448 | yowil | you will |
| 1451 | disgest | digest |
| 1460 | poraige | potage |
| 1488 | hord | herde |
| 1511 | greeuious | greeuous |
| 1516 | al redy linkt | readie linkt |
| 1520 | *Lomia* | *Lomie* |
| 1540 | bred | breede |
| 1541 | ha alas | alas |
| 1542 | fsming | fomyng |
| 1549 | fince | since |
| 1568 | bring you such | bryng suche |
| 1579 | a pace | apace |
| 1584 | whither | whether |
| 1585 | my owne decay | myne owne decaie |
| 1586 | and shall | and it shall |
| 1587 | pretendeth | pretended |
| 1588 | *Card*. hee | *Cardolus* he |
| 1593 | els but to | els to |
| 1610 | Ioging | ioggyng |
| 1616 | by your leaue | be your leaue |
| 1645 | foundling | fondlyng |
| | dewtifull | duetifully |
| 1664 | stlll | still |
| 1680 | with out | without |
| 1682 | Oo more | No (catchword for missing sig. G1ʳ) |

# APPENDIX

In the following transcriptions printed material which has been deleted or altered is set in italic and followed by a closing square bracket. Angle brackets indicate text difficult or impossible to decipher; dots within angle brackets stand for the illegible characters (⟨..⟩). Deletions of manuscript material are placed within square brackets.

1. The first set of interlineated manuscript annotations to Q1 *Common Conditions* is to Lamphedon's speech on C1ʳ and Clarisia's speech on C2ᵛ. Written in black ink and in secretary hand, these notes transform the words of the play's characters to describe the love of a Suffolk youth for his mistress, 'Anne' or 'Agnis'.

C1ʳ Lamphedon's speech

| | |
|---|---|
| 524 | *what he was*] deleted; replaced with *ye mind of him* |
| 526 | *his*] deleted; replaced with *my* |
| 528 | *Aple*] *A* and *e* struck through |
| | *lady*] *l* struck through |
| 532 | *Lamphedon*] lightly struck out; replaced with *Amos* |
| 533 | *Lady*] deleted; replaced with *a mayden* |
| 534 | *sonne to the Duke of Phrygia*] deleted; replaced with *so* ⟨*cl...*⟩ *wt cares* ⟨*.e*⟩ *[ as any in this ] be so foyld as any in this so* |
| | The annotator has extensively revised this line to read: *Shalt thou which art so* ⟨*clere*⟩ *wt cares be so foyld as any in this so noble soyle.* |
| 535 | *to* inserted at beginning of line |
| 536 | *Phrygian ladies here*] deleted; replaced with *maides of suffolk soile* |
| 537 | *foraine dame*] deleted; replaced with *maiden now* |
| 539 | *marsiall feats*] deleted; replaced with *pleasure great* |
| | *knight*] deleted; replaced with *love* |

C2ᵛ Clarisia's speech

| | |
|---|---|
| 638 | *my hand here houering stands, to writ some prety verse to thee* \| *my morning mynd for to delight that wante the Ioyes that be* inserted above Clarisia's entrance |
| 639 | *for as yᵉ* inserted above the beginning of the line |

Tucker Brooke reads this as 'for us y(?)', seeing it as an unfinished last clause of the annotation inserted at TLN 638. However, a comparison between the 'a' here and the a's in 'hand' and 'stands' in that annotation suggests that the word is 'as', not 'us'. The annotator probably intended the words to begin the line as 'for as y^e lewred hauke . . .'

641–2    The annotator has revised these lines extensively and they should probably read: *So I through loue of thee my deare who hath my hart in hold, | Haue fixt my eye, vntill I die, thou maist be sure and bold*

641    *sight*] deleted; replaced with *loue*
     *valiant knight*] deleted; replaced with *thee my deare who hath my* [⟨p..ect⟩ *euen*] *hart in hold*

642    *vppon Lamphedon*] deleted; replaced with *the sweet* [⟨ug.⟩] *Anne most thou maist be sure and bold* inserted at end of line

643    *valiant knight*] deleted; replaced with *my sweet hart*

647    *Lamphedon*] struck out; replaced with *sweet Agnis*

652–3    *whom all y^e maids of suffolke soyle could once cause the* [*once*] *to rue | but thou sweet Anne hath compelld me thy sweet loue for to sue* inserted, with a horizontal caret, between these lines and written in the outer margin of the page. 652 *once* inserted above caret; [*once*] inserted above caret; 653 *for* inserted

653    *thou forcedst me to loue*] deleted; replaced with *it is thy will o loue thou* inserted after *ha*

654    *his*] deleted; replaced with *thy*

654–5    *therfore sweet Agnis ꝑ pend this well whiles I do lyue in Ioy | none other shall attayne my loue, though it bred myne anoy* inserted, with a horizontal caret, between these lines and written in the lower margin of the page

655–6    struck through

655    *Clarisia*] deleted; replaced with *Amos*
     *he is a duke his sunne*] partially deleted; replaced with *thou art but a poore mans sonne*

656    *thou but*] deleted; replaced with *she*
     *a knight, of meaner state*] deleted; replaced with *one that is rich & of better*
     *art*] replaced with *to*

2. The second set of interlineated annotations, to Sabia's speeches on C4^r, C4^v, and D2^r, transform Sabia's words in order to reflect a lady's love for her 'Edward'. They are in secretary hand, but are far less legible than the earlier

set of annotations. This is largely due to the fact they were written in brown ink that is much lighter than the earlier black one. These annotations may possibly be in a different hand from the earlier. They certainly appear to be scrawled much more quickly and haphazardly than the annotations to Lamphedon's and Clarisia's speeches. Against the hypothesis that these are two different hands stands the fact that the lines annotated in Sabia's speeches are often very similar (or even identical) in effect to those annotated in the earlier speeches, as are the changes made. TLN 909 is, moreover, the line 'borrowed' by the earlier annotator in his interlineations between TLN 654 and 655. If the annotations are by the same hand, the second set was unquestionably made with less care.

C4ʳ Sabia's speech

754    *sweet Nomides*] replaced with *Edward Dear*
757    *him*] replaced with *the*
758    *his*] replaced with *thy*
766    *a princes for to bee*] replaced with *in Riche a state to be*
768    *Phisicions*] deleted; replaced with *poore mans*

C4ᵛ Sabia's speech

770    *knight*] replaced with *loue*
771    *comlines*] replaced with *gentilnes*
       *the knights of Phrygia rowt*] replaced with *all yong men here about*

D2ʳ Sabia's speech

904    *A wo be to the time that*] deleted; replaced with *[th⟨...⟩]* beneath the line
905    *a* inserted before line
       *my*] deleted
       *& Ioy* inserted after *hope*
       *whom*] deleted; replaced with *wᶜh*
909    *Ah sir Nomides*] replaced with *therefore Edward perpend this well*

G4ᵛ (see Introduction p. xxi)

The final annotation, which appears after the printer's decorative ornament on the quarto's last page, is written in black ink and in italic hand with some secretary characters.

*Etsi (m.p.) hæc fabula*

    *(m<sup>r</sup> p)*

*Etsi est ⟨.⟩ ἔωλος hæc fabula præsertim tantis novis rebus: tamen
perire meam lucubrationem nolui*

# An excellent and pleasant Comedie, termed after the name of the Vice,

Common Condicions, drawne out of the most famous historie of *Galiarbus* Duke of *Arabia*, and of the good and æuill successe of him and his two children, Sedmond *his sun*, and Clarisia *his* daughter: Set foorth with delectable mirth, and pleasant shewes.

## ¶The Players names.

The Prologue.
Galiarbus, the olde duke of Arabia.
Sedmond, his sun.
Clarisia, his daughter.
Common Condicions, the Vice.
Shift.
Drift. } 3.Tinkers,
Vnthrift.
Metrea, a mayde.
Leostines, a knight that loueth Metrea.
Lamphedon, a knight that loueth Clarisia, and fighteth for her.
Nomides, a knight that loueth Metrea.
Cardolus, a knight that fighteth with Lamphedon.
M. of the ship.
Masters Mate. } 4. Mariners.
Boateswayne.
Shipboy.
Mountagos, a Spaniard.
Sabia, his daughter.
Lomia, a naturall foole.

Six may play this Comedie.

¶Imprinted at London by William How, for Iohn Hunter, dwellynge on London Birdge, at the signe of the Blacke Lion.

1

# ¶ The Prologue.

Y Ou skilfull heads, that sit in place to sée, likewise to heare,
    What openly by Actours déeds in place shall straight appeare:
Béfore your vigill wakefull eyes therfore perpend it well.
For the acts in order follow, which the preface may not tell.
But thus I shew, most strange it is, and pittifull beside,
Mixt both w mirth, & pleasant showes: wherfore we pray you bids
The last as well as first to sée, then vprightly iudge and way
Our Authors minde and doyng his, in that which wee display.

Let iudgement then from you procéde discréetly to be showne,
And let not rashnes ouerswne to mutch abroade be blowne.
For thus wée do perswade our selues, if simple Authors skill
Should Seneca exéede in verse, or Ouids pleasant quill:
Or could tell more then Tullies wit, eke Homer put a side,
Yet do wée déeme some Momus would him skorne, mocke, & deride.
But as he doth déepe low descend from these right famous wights:
So doth he stand in redines to bare those Momus spights.
Yet staies him on this steadfast hope, the wise his simple paine
Will well except, and that is all that hée doth séeke to gaine.

Let this for preface you suffice, the actours redy stand,
Your patience ernestly wée craue to procéde out of hand.

    ¶Here entreth Galiarbus, with Sedmond,
      and Lady Clarisia.

M Y children both, whose aged Syer from natiue soyll must pas,  Galiarb
    To lead his life in forraine Lands, for in vaine tis a las
To craue of king Arbaccus hée, in Arabia to remaine,
Wheras your aged mother shée her corpes in earth hath laine.
Sutch was the spight of Parasites, so is dame fortune straunge
That I from out Arabia must in other cuntreis range.
And this the last day is you sée, that I may here remaine
With you my children both alas, which causeth mée complaine
With trebell care and penssiuenes, ha all my only ioy,
The sight of you doth cause me now to waile with great annoy.
And therfore my sonne Sedmond now on this my blessinge here,
I charge thée to remaine for aye true to thy sister dere.

                   A ii           Be

Be thou a stay, to her decay, a rocke and fortresse strong,
And do not see, her ennimy, to profer her sutch wronge.
Bée thou her shield, in towne and field, her fence and onely stay,
Let not her foe, procure her woe, I hartely thée pray.
Be thou her frénd, vnto the end, her faithfull brother true,
And graunt that shée, remaine with thée, lest doubtfull cares ensue.   40
Thus I thy sier, of thée require, as duty doth thée binde,
Let nature rule thée, to cherish her truly, and be to her most kinde.

mond.   Right louinge sier, whose charge well waid & lodged in my brest,
Whose minde as it did neuer swarue but yelded to your heste,
I am your Sedmond till I die, I am and will remaine
My sisters true and faithful frénd though I the death sustaine.
The charge that you haue geuen mée shalbe performed sure,
The wight that doth my sister wrong his death will I procure.   50
And therfore, my swéete louing sier, for vs take you no care,
The gods we trust shall vs defend, and rid from out their Snare.
But ha my father graunt that I thy Icarus may bée
To wend and dwell in woods and Caues to liue and die with thée.

rifia.   And graunt Galiarbus my swéet sire, that I with thée may goe,
And not for to remaine behind to waill with cares and woe.

liarbus.   Ha no my children, do refraine séeme not to craue of mée,
Do not betake your selues like case for banisht wights to bée.
Though Minos hee that cruell kinge did banish Dedalus,
And though your father is like case by this kinge Arbaccus?   60
Yet mought his Icarus remaine in Creta quietly
Where hée did passe his daies before hée practized to fly.
Wherfore my children, cease your talke, do not your father gréeue,
And séeme no more in any wise such question forth to méeue.
And now fare well, your aged sier no longer may remaine,
For that he is cast into exile from you his children twaine.

rifia.   O father, sith you will depart from hence your selfe alone,
Graunt that I may demaund of you but onely question one.

liarbus   Craue what thou wilt Clarisia, I graunt what so it bée.
rifia.   Then where ý mindst for to remaine god father shew to mée.
liarbus.   Where to remaine Clarisia, of truth I know not I.   70
rifia.   Then do thy children thée commend vnto the heauens hie,
Desseringe them most entirely to shield thée from all woe,

                                          And

# called Common condicions.

And bée to thee assistance good where thou doest ride or goe.    Exit.

Ha farwel farwel my childrē twain your sier must néds depart Galarib

Farewell O father, to thee againe the cause of this our smart.  Both spe

Clarisia, sith fortune hath to vs sutch lot assind,    Sedmon

In this our prime of yeres to part from parents both so kinde,

The one being bereft of life, as was the gods decree,

The other cast into ercile, a banisht knight to bee,

We must contente our selues with all, refraining wonted care,

In hope the gods for vs in time a salue will soone prepare.

Wherfore sister Clarisia, let vs againe retire

Unto our fathers mansion plase I hartely you desire.

Where wee will liue in quiet rest.

Ha cruell words to soone exprest.    Clarisia.

Ha brother Sedmond, how can you liue in quiet rest one day,

And seinge thus our father deere banisht from vs away,

Leaue of this fond request of thine, let pity pearce thy hart,

Sith nature can thee not constraine to waile thy fathers smart.

What ioy should I obtaine, alas, if I a princes were,

To see my father rainge abroad in cuntreies strange for feare?

Ha brother Sedmond leaue of this talke and blot it out of mind e

And be not found to father thine obliuious and vnkinde,

But be thou still right sorowful, and pensiue for his sake.

Why sister, what thought do you mean ȳ you would haue me take Sedmond

The griefe that I should take for him I see it were in vayne,

And not of force him to restore to natiue soyll againe.

And therfore my sweet sister dear refraine once more from talke,

And come let vs retire with speed, Let vs straight home go walke,

And let vs waile no more I pray.

Stay.    within    Condic.

Stay? wherfore should I stay?    Sedmond.

Lest thou woorke thy owne decay.    Condiciōs

Decay? how can I do so?    Sedmond.

Through force of thy fo.    Condiciōs

Of fo? come sister content yee.    Sedmond.

Nay, stay lest thou repent thee.    Condiciōs

Why should I repent mee? I haue not offended.    Sedmond.

If that thou retourne, thy death is pretended.    Condiciōs

A iij    Pre

5

A pleasant comedy,

**Edmond.** Pretended? ha gods, what haue I done that I should die therfore? `110`
Come forth I say what so thou be, and do reply no more.
If thou be an Ecco or Ghost in like case,
Come forth with speed draw nere into place.

**Conditiõs** I am neither Ghost, Spirit, Ecco, nor crier,
And neither fish nor flesh, but halfe a true knaue, halfe a lier.

**Edmond.** What taunting wight art thou that doest in Eccos sort reply?
By like thou art some Parasite come our talke for to descry.

**Condic.** Parasite? nay if there bee no remedy but needs enter I must,
I will to it with a good heart and lay all fear in the dust.

¶Here entreth Conditions. `120`

**Clarisia.** What Master Conditions, what newes at court this day?
**Conditiõs** Ha sutch newes that I am afraid will turne to your decay.
**Edmond.** What is that good Conditions I pray thee expresse.
**Conditiõs** Ha, I haue wept so that for faintnes the truth I cannot confesse.
**Clarisia.** Good Conditions leaue of thy wayling and shew the matter.
**Conditiõs** Ha, a vengance of all villaines that would seeme for to clatter,
Ha, that same king Arbaccus by parasits is so allured,
That your deathes all ready hee hath procured.
If that you seeme to retire backe againe, `130`
The king hath layd waite that you both mought be taine,
And so conuaied to some prison away,
Where he doth intend to worke your decay.
Auoid all sutch dangers if you will be ruled by mee,
Seeme not to retire againe, but in continent fly.
And so shall you be sure your liues for to saue
Though they amongst them your goods chance to haue,
And I will fly with you as a seruant to bee,
If with a good will you willingly entertaine mee.
**Edmond.** Yes with a good will, Conditions, with all our hart, `140`
And therfore straitwaies let vs hence depart.
**Clarisia.** Ha cruell kinge Arbaccus thou, ha tiger fierce vntame,
That first our fathers banishment procuredst for to frame.
And that thou art not pleased with all but seekest our decay.
Woe worth the time I first was borne, to see this dismall day.
Euen as the wolfe, or tyger fierce doth seeke the lambe to kill:
So seekest thou both day and night our innocent blood to spill.

Ha,

6

Ha thou that banished haſt our ſire foz no offence at all,
But thzough thy flattering paraſites haſt wzought his end and fal.
A double woe remaine to thæ,ha cruell kinge vnkinde,
Graunt Priams ſtate to be his ſtate that ſuch daies hæ may finde.
And fare well now Arabia ſoile, fare well our natiue land,
Farewell all pompe and pleaſure eke , foz wæ haue taine in hand
To fly from you,wæ fozced are foz ſauegard of our liues,
To raing in cútreies ſtraing abzoad wher foztune foozth vs dziues.

   Clariſia leaue of your plaints an ruthfull griefes of minde,     Sedmon
And come let vs go rainge a bzoad our father foz to finde,
That we may háue his company in this our baniſhment.

   Pzocæde you when you pleaſe,to follow you I am content,     Clariſia.
And come Conditions wend with vs thy company let vs haue.     Exeunt.
   Kæpe on your way maddam, you næde it not to craue.     Condiciõ
Ha ha Conditions,φ you,there are two ſozts of cõditions as I ges.
Foz there are good and æuell conditions the truth to confeſſe.
And to which of theſe twaine thinke you diſpoſed am I?
If I ſhould ſay to good conditions you would reply.
On the contrary ſide,if I ſhould ſay to euell I did cleaue,
Then euery Jack would thzuſt me out of dozes ſtreight by ỹ ſlæue.
And therfoze foz my owne aduantage belæue me you may,
As nere as I can ile vſe a mediocritie by the way.
And Mediocritie is my name though condicions they mæ call,
Nere kinde to daine foztune to raiſe and to let fall.
As foz experience,it was my chance to bleſſe one the other day,
And within two dayes after hæ was hanged out of the way.
But to ſhow you the chiefe cauſe now wherfoze and why
This knight with his famelly are faine foz to fly,
I wil.There are certeine paraſites haunting the court night & day
With whom this knight Galiarbus could neuer away.
Hæ theſe paraſites perſued thzough his outward apperance,
Which cauſed them to hate him and theron wzought his græuance
Foz why they accuſed him of treaſon to Arbaccus the kinge,
Repozting him to bæ one that ſought the realmes vndoinge.
The which he neuer went about,but toke ſtill great paine
In kinge Arbaccus behalfe the realme to maintaine.
But I am the arrants villaine that you ſhall finde oz ſæ,

                                          Foz

For the baniſhment of Galiarbus was all longe of mee.
For ſecretly I ſet mee aparaſite him to accuſe,
That hee the common wealth ſought to abuſe.
Now had I tould the king before, how, and in what ſort
The accuſacion being red, that he would report.
Then ſtept I to Galiarbus, and rounded him in the eare,
Saying if he would put ẙ matter into my hands he nede not feare.    190
Now he being contented, I went to the kinge by and by,
And bid him aſke if hee were ſo content, and hee anſwered I.
Thinking the king aſked him if hee would that I in place
Should anſwere againſt his accuſers in his caſe.
But I had toulde the king ſutch a tale in his behalfe before,
That in faith hee neede not many accuſers more.
And ſo vpon his one anſwere he was condemned to dy.
Then I like a crafty knaue, ſtept forth by and by,
Deſiering the kinge not to put him to death out of hand :
But for ſo ſmall offence to baniſh him the land.    200
The knight hering mee to ſpake ſo in his cauſe,
Looke mee for his ſpeciall freend without farther pauſe.
And theron the kinge appointed him a day by and by
To depart the land, but taken after that day, he ſhould dy.
Now the kinge on the other ſide, perſeuinge my crafty fetch,
If hee could haue taken me I know that I ſhould ſtretch.
And ſo in faith there is no more cumming to the court for mee,
But how ſay you, haue not I deuiſd well to haue company?
For the kinge thought as mutch of theſe as of his death I am ſure,
But onely to haue their company this he I did procure.    210
Tuſh, this is but a pece of my conditions by the way.
But by your leaue I will vſe Amedyocritie whoſoeuer ſaies nay.
Well, there is no remedy, I muſt after thē their company to haue
For I am ſure that is all that they ſeeme for to craue.    Exit.

¶Here enter. 3. Tinkers, Shifte, Drifte,
and Vnthrifte, Singinge.

The tink-
ers ſonge.

Hay tiſty toſty tinkers good fellowes they bee,
In ſtopping of one hole they vſe to make three.

Come

COme merely foorth mates, and let the worlde wagge,
   Though our trade do decay our mirth shall augment.
This tinkerly trade wee geue it the bagge,
Like beggers wee liue and want to pay rent.
Yet wee neuer lin trudging from citie to towne,
Our hammers on the kettels bottomes do ringe :
Yet we scarse get lether piltches with out cloke or gown,
Fie on this trade that no more gaine will bringe.
     Hay tisty tosty Tinkers good fellowes they bee.
     In stopping of one hole they vse to make three.


     Shift he with shifting hath almost mard all,
He can not be trusted in no kinde of place:
For many olde things into his budgit doth fall,
That oft time he feareth to show forth his face.
Pots, Saucers, Candilsticks, and Scummers beside,
Are trust vp and closely layd into the packe:
Away hee hies quickly and dares not abide,
Shifts bandogge doth beare his tooles on his backe.
     Hay tisty tosty, Tinkers good fellowes we bee,
     wee stop one & make two, wee stop two and make three.


     Nay yet rather Drift is worthy of blame,
That is oft times driuen to a weake stay.
To rob, kill, and spoile, he taketh no shame,
Driuen for to get it, and to haue no nay
And vnthrift againe consumes it as flat
Weemen, dise and drinke, lets him nothing keepe:
And therfore all wee three haue met together pat,
To venture a robbing, to play now bo peepe.
     Hay tisty tosty , Tinkers good fellowes they bee,
     They stop one hole, make two and stop two & make three.


                         B.          Hey

Shift. HEy liuely, by gogs bloud wee tinkers are at a mad ſtay,      (day
For whē we are in ẏ city, there is nothing but tinkel tinke al ẏ

Drift. And by gogs bloud Shift, I can not go but my baſſon muſt tang :
And by your leaue if I had not deuiſd this drift, I mought go hang.

Vnthrift. And by his woūds my Maſters I am in ẏ ſame ſtate you twain be
But whē folke bring their kettels to mēd for one hole I make thrēe
But my maſters wot you what ? I heard newes about ẏ court this
That there is a gentleman with a Lady gone away,      (day
And haue with them a litle paraſite, full of mony and quoine.
By gogs bloud let vs leaue of tinking and follow them to purloine.
For the littell knaue hath got it with cogging, and telling of tales.
And therfore by my conſent with his quoine we wil fill our males.

Shift. Felow Vnthrift by gogs bloud here is my hand on ẏ condicion,
Wee wil take away their purſes and ſay we do it by commiſſion.
But by his wounds, although I haue no commiſſion to ſhowe
I intend not to let them part with their purſes I trowe.

Drift. A commiſſioner gogs bloud who made a commiſhoner of you?
If ẏ haue no better anſwer at the bar ẏ wilt hange I tel thēe trew.

Shift. Hang you tinkerly ſlaue? Shift wil ſcape whē Drift ſhalbe hāged

Vnthrift. Tuſh my maſters you are bothe as good as euer twanged,

Drift. I pray thēe, good Vnthrift ſtand back, ẽ let me try with ẏ ſlaue.

Shift. If thou dareſt Ile lay my hammer on your pate you knaue.

Vnthrift. My Maſters leaue of your brawling thus one with an other.

Drift. By gogs bloud I cannot hold my hands ẽ if hēe were my brother.
You howreſun Banbery ſlaue, come againe and thou dare.

Shift. By his woūds, to hurle my kettel at thy hed I take no great care

Drift. And if thou hurle thine, thinke not but againe
Both ſkillet, baſſon, and hamer ſhall at thy hed amaine.
And therfore by gogs bloud hurle and thou dare.

Shift. If thou do begin, then hange mēe and I ſpare,

Vnthrift. Well then my maſters to it with a good will, and neuer care.

they fight. And I will play on my kettell as though I were a drumſtare.
Stay, ſtay, no more brawling now one with another.

Shift. By gogs bloud Drift, Ile breake your noddell if you were my
And thou be a honeſt fellow Thrift let vs but try      (brother.

Drift. Come and thou dare, for I pas not a turd for thee I.

Vnthrift. Leaue of this brawling my maſters, and heare what I ſhall ſay,
The Gentelman with his lady intend to come this way,

And therfore let vs be all in one minde, and agre all together,
For I know it will not be long oz they come hether.
And therfore let vs be packing hence, and in a buſh ly,
Untill they be already to pas a long hereby.

**290**

And when they thinke themſelues in the wood moſt ſureſt to bée:
Their purſes wée will bée ſo bolde as ſhare betwirt vs thrée.
How ſay you my maſters how like you this deuiſe?
  By gogs bloud fellow thrift thou art ercellent wiſe.          Shift.
Well fellow drift becauſe of our buſines I thée forgiue,
And Ile make thee amends and we both ſkape the gallous & llue.
  Shift this is your knauery if you breake ones hed with a pan,  Drift.
You will giue him a plaiſter to hele it againe if you can.
Well here is my hand, I forgiue thée with all my hart,

**300**

  Well come on then, in continent let vs from hence depart.      Shift.
    ¶Here enter, Sedmond with Clariſia                            Exeunt
      and Condicions out of the wood.                             omnes.
THe ſilly traueiler that vs atachd through weried toyle,         Sedmon
    And forſt through meare neceſſity to trace from natiue ſoyle,
Though weried at his iournies end with painfull traueill paſt:
Is glad in hart he hath attaind his iournies end at laſt.
So we beinge poſſeſt as now with weried toile like caſe,
Muſt liue in hope all traueill paſt to finde a reſting place.
Wherfore good ſiſter be of chere caſt care from out your minde,

**310**

And liue in hope all ſorowes paſt our father out to finde.
You ſée the chirpping birds beginnes you mellody to make,
But you vngrateful vnto them their pleaſant voice forſake.
You ſée the Nightingall alſo, with ſwéete and pleaſant lay,
Sound forth her voice in cherping wiſe, to baniſh care away.
You ſee dame Tellus ſhée, with mantell freſh and gréene,
For to diſplay euery where moſt cumly to be ſéene.
You ſée dame Flora ſhée, with flowers freſh and gaye
Both here and there and euery where her banners to diſplay,
Wherfore good ſiſter caſt of care, abiect this griefe of minde,

**320**

In hope the gods for this our ſore a ſalue no doubt will finde.
  Brother Sedmond, the traueiler deſerueth place of reſt,        Clariſia.
In that hee taken hath ſutch paines as you before erpreſt.
But brother wee are no trauellers that vſeth day by day,

                              B y                                 To

I I

To rainge abroad to foraine Lands to trace the beaten way.
Wée are constraind through very force to fly from natiue soyle,
Wée are compeld through cruelty to vnder take this toile.
The traueiller may kéepe the way that likes him best to go.
Wée are constraind to shrowd our selues in woods for feare of fo.
Then brother tell me whether he or we do take most paine,
Considering when he please he may returne to home againe?

You say the Nightingall also with swéete and pleasant lay,
Doth sound her notes in chirpinge wise to banish care away.
What pleasure may wée take in her or in quéene Flora shée?
What pleasure in dame Tellus eke thinke you for vs to bée?
No no god brother Sedmond, their pleasant noyse they make,
Would rather cause me as I am all pleasure to forsake.
What pleasure should we take brother, if all the birds in field
Were present here at instance now their harmony to yéeld?
Their pleasant voice renewes my care, their swete melodious soūd
Doth cause me now with trickling teares in sorrowes to abound.
For thinking on the pleasures now that earst in time we had:
Doth cause me now to pine for wo wher hart would haue me glad
And therfore brother leaue of talke, in vaine you séeme to prate,
Not all the talke you vtter can my sorrowes can abate.
From sutch vaine allegations, good brother séeme to stay.

*Condi.*   Nay noble gentelman vnder your correction if I may,
I haue a woord or two with your sister by the way.
How say you Lady Clarisia, are you like case contented?

*Clarisia.*   Conditions if thou speake thy minde it shall not bée repented.

*Condi.*   Then in your quarrell against your brother I minde to breake
So that with licence gentleman you wil giue me leaue to speake.

*Sedmond.*   With a good will Conditions, speake forth what is thy minde.

*Conditiōs.*   Then in faith Ile pay some home anon in their right kinde.
It is geuen to wéemen to be obscure & ful of simpricty by the way
Proffer them the thing they most desier they wold it denay.
They are so full of sleights and fetches that scarce the Fox hée,
In euery poinct with wéemen may scarce compared bée,
For when men pray they will denay, or when men most desire:
Then marke me a woman she is sonest stirred vnto ire.
Their heds are fantasticall and full of variety strange,

Like

Like to the Moone whose operation it is often times to change.
And by your leaue howsoeuer it goes the mastery they must haue,
In euery respect or in ought that they seeme for to craue.
But Madam, I hope you will inpute no blame vnto mée,
Considering you are a mayden, and full of imbycillity.
  A well Master Conditions, is this my part you take so? Clarisia
  Mistresse Clarisia, to my powre the truth I must show. Condi¿
  Of truth Conditions the truth thou hast tolde Sedmo
  Nay and shall please you I am some what feminatiue, Condi¿
For if there be any thing in minde out I must it driue.
  Down with them all for surely they shall die, Shift.
  Ah cruell chance, good brother fly. Clarisia
  Why where is the other that was in their company? Drift.
By gogs bloud minks hée shal bie his flying full deare.
  And in faith you wiseld faced knaue, ere you part from hence, Thrift
Ile be so bolde as diue in your pocket to share out your pence.
  Nay gentelmen Tinkers, be good vnto vs twaine. Condit
  Make and end, take away all they haue I say once againe. Shift.
  Ah cruell luckles chaunce alas, ah fortune thou vnsure, Clarisia
That canst in turning of thy whéele still cause vs to endure
Sutch changed heaps of woes (alas) as tongue cannot expresse:
For why I see in vayne it is as now to séeke redresse.
Wherfore you cruell Tyrants thrée, dispatche my life in haste,
For why I Ioy no longer life sutch heapes of greif I taste.
  Tush dispatch, and when you haue done, binde her fast to this trée. Drifte.
Least when y we are gone she make an vprore, and we persaed bée
  Come on Lady, fast to this trée, we intend you to binde. Shift
And with your owne handcarcher your eies wée will blinde.
  So in faith minks you are fast now for skaping away, Thrifte
  A wo be to the time when first I saw this luckles day. Clarisia
  Why what shall we do with him by gogs bloud I can not deuise Thrifte
Except we should set him to kepe crowes, & picke out both his eies.
  Ah of all loues haue compassion on mée and serue me not so. Condi¿
Here ye? and you can not tell what to do with mée, then let mée go.
The diuell a peny haue I, and you will hang me on this trée.
  Gogs bloud and well sayd, for he hath red his owne destinie. Shifte.
  Ha, will you let me go? in good faith thanke you I do, Condie
  Nay, stay a while, we tell thée not so. Drittea

13

For thou art like now to hang on this trée.

*ondiciōs*   Ha and there be no remedy but hanged I must bée

One of you hange befoze to show howwell it will become mée.

*hrifte.*   To hang thée oz sutch as thou art, we thinke it but a spozt.

*ondiciōs*   Cast not away a propor young man in sutch a kinde of sozt.

*ifte.*   Tush dispatch and hange him straight out of the way.

*ondiciōs*   Ha good gentelman Tinker, I beséech you now stay,

What meane you by his wounds I haue beraied my self out of cry

*rift.*   Whether thou hast oz hast not thou shalt surely dy.

*ondiciōs*   Ha and there be no remedy but that néeds hang I must,

Giue me the halter Ile to it my selfe and lay all care in the dust.

*hrifte.*   I am sure thou meanest not to hange without helpe of a frénde

*ditions*   Ist not as good to hang my selfe as another hale the end?

*ifte.*   By gogs bloud my Masters and hée will we are all content,

Foz then in time foz hanging him we néede not repent.

Well Drift giue the halter vnto the elfe.

*ondiciōs*   Ha was there euer littell knaue driuen to hang himselfe?

Nay I must also request your ayd to helpe me into the trée.

*drifte.*   Nay if thou lacke any helpe, then hange vs all thrée.

So law now dispatch, and with spéede make an ende,

*ondiciōs*   What to do?     Drift, Mary to hang thy self

*ondiciōs,*   Nay by your leaue that is moze then I do intend.

*hrift.*   Why I am sure thou intendest not to serue vs in such sozt?

*ondiciōs*   Were not hée mad would hang himself to show thrée tinkers spozt?

*ife.*   Why I am sure to serue vs so, thou dost not intend?

*ondit.*   A mad foole hée were would desperatly dy and neuer did offend,

*rifte.*   By gogs bloud Ile teare him downe oz els Ile léese my life.

*ondit.*   Backe againe oz ile be so bould as pare your nails w' my knife.

*hrifte.*   Nay loke my masters the slaue lookes like an owle in a trée,

*ifte.*   Nay hée lookes like a crafty knaue beléeue mée.

*rift.*   By gogs bloud Shift he lookes like a madge howlet as ÿ hast said

By the mas if I had my bow and boult here hee should be payd.

*ondi.*   Halo, halo halo, howe.      holoweth in the tree.

*hrift.*   Why, what doost thou meane to hollow in the trée?

*ondi.*   What do I meane mary to haue moze company come to mée.

*ifte.*   By gogs bloud my masters we were not best lōger here to stay,

*anob,*   I thinke was neuer sutch a crafty knaue befoze this day, Exeunt.

Are

14

Are they all gone? ha ha ha, welfare olde shift at a neede,
By his woundes had I not deuised this I had hanged indeede.
Tinkers (quoth you) tinke mée no tinks Ile meddel wͨ thē no moꝛe
I thinke was neuer knaue so vsed by a companie of tinkers befoꝛe
440    By your leaue Ile be so bould as to looke about me and spy,
Least any knaues foꝛ my cumming downe in ambush do ly.
By your licence I minde not to pꝛeache longer in this tree.
My tinkerly slaues are packed hence as far as I may see.
Ha, my good mistres Clarisia, I am soꝛy to se you at this stay,
I will vnbinde you that we may in all the haste trudge away.
And Lady it is not best foꝛ vs in Arabia longer to tary,
Seeing that foꝛtune in euery respect against vs still doth varie.
Foꝛ seeing wee are so ny the sea that wee may pas in one day
450    Cleane ouer the sea to Phrygia, I would not wish wee stay
Whereas now your good father sir Galiarbus is,
And of your bꝛother I warrant you wee there shall not misse.
    Wel, sith néeds wee must, I am content to foꝛtunes beck to bow
Whom showes her self an enemie to me poꝛe wꝛetche as now.
Wherefoꝛe a dew Arabia soyle, farwell my bꝛother deare,
It boutles is, I sée, as now in woods to séeke thée heare.
    Well Lady, without any farther talke let vs away.
    Pꝛocéede Condicions, I minde not here in danger longe to stay.
                                                    Exeunt.

        ¶Here entreth Sedmond waylyng.
T He wyght that had a Iuell fayꝛe and by misfoꝛtune strainge,
460        Thꝛough negligence hath lost the same, as he abꝛode did rainge,
The iewell beyng none of his, but ones that was his freend,
Who did the same béetake to him from losses to defend:
Now being lost, thꝛough negligence of him that kept the same,
What double greif thinke you doth he within his bꝛest stil frame?
My sister shee the iewell is, whom father gaue to mee
Foꝛ to pꝛeserue from cruell foe, within my garde to bee.
But I (alas) thꝛough negligence haue lost my sister deere
Thꝛough cruell tyꝛants furious foꝛce within this foꝛest heere,
But ha my sister, is this thy chance that foꝛtune hath assinde?
470    Must thou alas to'rapin yéeld? must thou now rest behinde?
Ha, why did I not béetake to flight the coꝛpes that liues in thꝛall?

                    B4

                    15

Why did I not with thée like case into their clutches fall?
Would gods Lucina she with sharpe and crooked crabbed knife,
When first I cam into this world had end my vitall life.
But sith it was not destinie, nor yet the gods decrée:
With this most wretched state(alas) I must contented bée.
But farewell now my Coursers braue, atrapped to the ground,
Farewell adew all pleasure eke, with cumly Hauke and Hound.
Farewell ye Nobels all, farewell eche Marsiall knight,
Farewell ye famous Ladies all, in whom I did delight.
A dew my natiue soyle, a dew Arbaccus kynge,
A dew eche wight, and Marsiall knight, a dew eche liuyng thynge.
A dew my wofull Sier, and Sister in like case,
Whom neuer I shall see agayne, eche other to embrace:
For now I will betake my selfe a wandryng knight to bee.
Into some straunge & forrayne land their cumly guise to see.  Exit.

¶Here entreth Galiarbus out of Phrygia.

Galiarbus.
WHo can but smyle and laugh to see the state of Fortune thée?
    Who can deuise in rightist wise, to yélde dew praise to thee?
Ha Goddisse y whose countnance straunge doth eb & flow eche day,
Sometimes thou doest restore to wealth, and sometime to decay.
As profe is playnly séene by mee, though banisht wight I was,
Thou hast restorde to wealth agayne, far better in eche case.
Though kynge Arbaccus hee, withall his courtly trayne,
And eke his route of Parasites, did holde mee in disdayne:
Yet through thy turnyng whéel, and variable chaynge,
Hast mée restord to wealth agayne in forayne countreis straynge.
How should I duly laud your names O heauenly powers for this?
How should wee giue you half the prayse that you deserue Iwis?
Sith that our mortall tongue vnable is to showe
The prayses that you ought to haue, which for our part wee owe,
Galiarbus shall not cease whilst life hee doth enioye:
In rightist wise he can deuise your prayses to imploye.
For why, though I but knight in Arabia did remayne:
It was my chaunce and fortune good here in Phrygia for to gayne
A Lordship great, the which the Duke hath now bestowd on mée,
Vpon condicion to remayn his subiect true to bée.

The

480

490

500

The which if I Galiarbus be euer falsely found.
Ye heauenly powres do all agrée my life to confound.
But am constraind in spight of force my wonted name to hide,
Least by that king Arbaccus spyes my state should be espide.
But ha Galiarbus,in this thy ioye what sorrowes doth abound?
What suddaine griefes atacht thy minde? what care thy hart doth
What good can all this liuing do to thee in forrain land, (wound?
And seing children twaine remaine as yet in tirants hand?
And in vaine tis to send for them,for why,that cruell kinge
For mine offence, I this am sure, in prison will them sling.
Well,of force I must content my selfe , and liue in care and woe,
From children twaine I must refraine,and for aie them forgoe.

¶Here enter Lamphedon out of Phrygia.

AS one that saw an aple faire in top of trée so hye,
   And durst not once presume to come , nor draw the same anye,
For that he knew not what he was that owd the péece of ground
Wherin the Aple on top of thée,in beauty did abound.
Which was a cause of his distres and double griefe of minde,
For that the kéepers of the same did show themselues vnkinde.
This Aple is a lady faire whome I espied this day,
As I in Forest hunting was persuing of the pray.
Whose bewty hath bewitched me,euen mawger Dians chase
To yéeld and be a courtier now vnto dame Venus grace.
Ha Lamphedon,where is become thy stout couragious minde?
Shall sight of Lady cause thee now to lead a life so blinde?
Shalt thou which art sonne to the Duke of Phrygia noble soyle,
Refraine thy woonted pleasures past,and vndertake this toyle?
Not all the Phrygian ladies here could cause thee for to rue,
Ha wretch,and hath a forrine dame compeld thee then to sue?
And must I yéeld in spight of force vnto Cupido hée?
And must I leaue my martiall feats to craue her knight to bée,
Whom neuer yet I saw before? ha cruell wretch vnkinde
To shote that dart to pearce my hart,why shouldst thy self so blind
I am to craue her loue(alas)whom neuer yet I sawe
To show like loue to mée againe,but did herselfe withdraw.
And this the first time is (alas) of her I had a sight,
Whose cumly lokes & bewty braue hath wrought to me this spight

C        Ha

Ya lady braue, would gods thou knewest the loue J beare to thee.
Would gods ÿ wretch would cause thee beare again like loue to me
Why Lamphedon, ÿ knowest not what she is perchãce a princesse
Ya cruel words, I thē am sure shee will holde me in skorne (borne
How dare I then attempt the thing:how dare I then be bolde?
How dare I once presume to her my sorrowes to vnfolde?  — 550
Would god when first I tooke my way the pleasant chase to vew:
I had bin slaine through cruell paine, then should not this insewe.
Would gods these eies of mine,which giues my body light,
When first they vewed thy comely grace they had bin pluckte out
For if Apelles hee were present here in place, (quite.
Vnpossible it were aright to picture forth thy grace.
But sith that Cupid will not force her for to yæld mee loue:
Would gods by other practices her answeres I might proue.
Or by some secret way and hidden strange deuice.  — 560

¶Here enter conditions standing priuely.

ndi. TO meddle with witchcrafte I count you not wise.
mphe. What wight art thou that answerest me in such a kinde of sort
ndi. It is hard winning of the city without skaling the fort,
mphe. Skalinge the forte? I go not about the citie to win.
ndi. Yæa but as far as I can sæ,Cupid hath hit the pin.
mphe. What wight art thou that in such sort dost sæme for to reply?
ndi. Hæ that is by Cupid possest of force must sorrow try.
mphe. I here a voice correcting,yet no liuing wight I sæ,  — 570
ndi. Hæ that trusts to a broken bough,may hap to fall from the trée.
mphe. Ya wretch what so thou bee, I would I had thee here,
ndi. In vaine tis when the dogs are wery to wish after the deare.
mphe. Nay sure,wretche,if I had thee heare thou forsytt me to do it,
ndi. Nay with a good will I besæke you spare not go to it,
But if I should stur euer a foote from this place,
Hæ might soone spy me,and then after me would he apace.
There is no remedy but to him I must and banysh feare away,
For in vaine it is from hence to depart or the foole to play.
Ya noble Gentleman god saue your life for euer to remaine.
mphe. Welcome my frænd didst thou reply when I did late complain  — 580
ndi. No gentleman I am no such felow as you take me for J,
He deserues death that any gentlemans talke would so descry.

18

Of truth if that I had him here his death he sure should gaine. Lamph
And worthy for deriuinge suche a gentleman to be slaine. Condi.
If he knew that I had answered him contrary to euery word
Hée would go nere to thrust me through ÿ buttoks with his sword.
But let Conditions alone howsoeuer this geare falles out,
Hée will vse a pollecy to bring this matter well about.
Now this geare cottons law, now shall you plainly sée,
Which waies so euer the winde blowes it is for my commoditie.
Ha noble gentleman, I am sory to se you at this stay,
That at the first sight of a Lady you should thus pine away.

Why good fellow how knowest thou my griefe, to mee expres?
Hée that hath felte loues bitter stormes must nœdes the truth Lamph
And hast thou bin a louer? I pray thée now declare. (confesse Condi.
Who I? that haue I bin in loue with my owne mothers mare Lamph
But what say you to him that would help you vnto that dame? Condi.
Who causeth you this ruthfully these sorrowes for to frame.

What say I (quoth you) mary I say he is worthy to haue. Lamph
The thinge that with toung is vnpossible to craue.
But my friend I pray thée expresse and shew to me thy name.

Master Affection, noble gentleman, euen the very same, Condi.
Master Affection, ha ye gods, now se I if it you please, Lamph
It lieth in your hands my sorrowes for to ease.

Gentleman whatsoeuer lyes in my hand is to your ease. Condi.
Commaund me euen what you list and Ile do what I please.

What sayst thou? Lamph
I say commaund me what you lyst, and Ile do what you please. Condi.
I commaund thee to do nothing, but to aide me here in, Lamphe
That I the Ladies loue through thy help may but win.
Which if thou canst do through pollecy and skill.
Demaund what thou wilt thou shalt haue it at thy will.

If I can do it quoth you? what kinde of question is that? Condi.
Nay put away if, for I can do it, this is plaine and flat,
And therfore noble Lamphedon you shall wend with mee,
Where secretly you shall stand her person for to sée.
Then shall you heare by her communication their,
What good will affection can cause her for to beare.
Wherfore noble knight, come let vs away.

C ij                                    Procéd

19

Proceede affection, on thy way, for I minde not to stay.                    620
You are the better man, therefore you shall first proceede.
Tush, tush affection, all this courtesie doth not neede.        Exit.
Ha ha ha, this geare fauls out excellent well in deede.
Welfare a craftie knaue at a time of neede.
Affection quoth you, why? what a counterfeit knaue am I,
Thus vnder the title of affection, my condicions to apply?
As though it lay in me to cause sutche for to loue?
No no thereis a nother that this practise did proue.
For Clarisia seeyng this Lamphedon a huntyng in the chase,
Was nigh constrained through Cupids force to sue to him for grace    630
Now I commyng this wayes the game for to see,
Chaunced to heare him for hir sake in wofull state to bee.
I will bring them together sure how so euer it fauls out,
For at length it will redowne to my profit I do not doubt.
Roome for a turne coate, that will turne as the wynde,
Whom when a man thinkes surest he knowes not where to finde.
                                                                Exit
Here entreth Clarisia alone.

THe lewred hauke whose rowling eyes are fixt on Partredge fast
      And liues in hope her flight once tayne to win her pray at last :    640
So I through sight of valiant knight within this forest here,
Haue fixt my eye, vntill I die, vppon Lamphedon deere.
Ha valiant knight, whose comly corps hath won my hart for euer,
Whose sight hath prest my tender brest, that I shal fayl thee neuer.
What double greifs feele I for thee? what woes do I sustaine?
What heapes of care in tender brest for thy sweet sake doth rayne?
Ha Lamphedon, do pitie here thy captiue in this case.
And graunt that she obtayne of thee thy fauour and thy grace.
Let not blinde Cupid wrongfully on me his cunnyng showe,
Let not my loue forsaken be which I to thee do owe.                     650
Let not thy mynde cleane contrary be setled on another.
Ha Cupid blinded God of loue, take not the tone for tother,
Sith that thou forcedst me to loue, ha mightie gods graunt mee,
That I may once obtayne his loue, my linked spouse to bee.
But ha Clarisia, thy talke is vayne, he is a duke his sunne,
And thou but daughter to a knight, of meaner state art come.
                                                                    He

He forceth not thy loue, he wayes not thy good will,
Wherfore refrayne with cruell payne, and liue as louer still.
 ¶Here entreth Lamphedon sodenly.
     What nædeth further trial then, when Judge hath heard ỹ tale? Lamph
what næds there further plée in case, when agræments doth assaile
what needs the Turtell with her mate, & she in place doth stande?
what need haue knights for Lady sights, to raynge in foraine land?
what næde I for to [ue] to thée thy loue for to obtayne,
O Lady deare, and séeyng that for me thou doest complayne?
Lamphedon doth professe he will to thee bee faithfull knight,
Not once for to forsake thy loue, for wronge ne yet for right.
And therfore Lady yælde to mee like promise here agayne,
To rest to me as I to thee, a louer true certayne.
wherfore O lady answer mee to this my question straight.
     The silly fish that once is tayne, must yæld vnto the bayght.  Clarisia
wherfore sir Knight right welcome sure vnto Clarisia shée,
who almost felt of Plutos paynes, and all for loue of thée.
If all the Troian knights were here, or Grecian in like case,
whose valiant courage did surpas eche wight in every place:
Clarisia doth protest, as she is Lady true,
To rest thy loue while life indure hap so what shall ensue.
And therfore my swéet louyng knight, haue no mistrust in mée,
For I do whole betake my selfe vnto the vse of thée.
So that thou wilt performe the bondes of wedlocke in this case,
I am content that none, but thou my corps shall sure iubrace.
wherfore sir Knight reply agayne, are you herein content?
     Else all the powers that sits in throne do end with cruell dent  Lamph
My youthfull dayes, and after that with Pluto let me rayne,
where as the greesly Hags do rest with trebell care and payne.
And therfore Lady, here is my hande, eke faith and trouth I giue,
To rest and be thy louing knight, whilst I haue day to liue.
In signe wherof take here this gim, and weare it for my sake.
     Upon condicion noble knight, the same of thée I take.  Clarisia
But yet receiue of Lady thine a pledge for pledge agayne,
In token that for aye I rest thy loue without disdayne.
The whiche Bracelet is made of golde, receaue that with good wil
And all that doth belong to me, shall rest as thine owne still.
                C iij          wherfore

Wherfore syr knight receiue the same of me thy lady deare,
 I shall O Lady for your sake euen place it present here.

And till I die I surely will weare it for loue of thine,
 And this shall rest in keping mine till dayes my life desine.

Well Lady then, my wife you are before the gods you see,

 I am and will remaine my deare a true Penelopæ.

Though I for thy sweete sake my knight a thousand woes should    **700**
 I would remaine as true to thee as shee did to her loue. (proue:

 And Lady, as true will I still rest to thee,
As Leander did that swome ouer the sea.
Wherfore O Lady wend with me vnto my fathers place,
Where wee will sone there marryed be if that the powres graunt
Wherfore my deare Clarisia, let vs no longer stay, (grace.

 To follow you whereso it bee, Clarisia shall obay.
Therfore proceed when you thinke best,

 To wayght vpon Clarisia Lamphedon aye is prest. Exeunt
  ¶Here enter Conditions sodeinly.         **710**

God giue you Ioy I hartely pray, and send you both good lucke,
 And if I might you should be sure to haue hornes like a Bucke.

Why how now Conditions, wher hast thou bin all this while?

Ha I chanst to fall a slepe as I was lifting my legge ouer a stile

And was that the matter thou staiedst so longe behinde?

In faith I haue slept so long that both mine eies are almost blind

What Master affection, of troth you are welcome, how fare you

Euen in good health noble gentleman, how do you? (now?

Affection, ye are misformed Conditions is his name.

By ȝ mas except I answere wisely it will tend to my shame.

I am sure his name is affection, let him deny it if he will,

Vnto any of those two names I must needs answere still.    **720**
For Affection my sure name is, this is plaine,
But Conditions my kirsun name is, to either of these twaine
Answere I will though it turne to my griefe,
Beleeue me gentleman, if I lie hange me like a theife.

 Nay wee beleeue thee Conditions without farther talke.

Well then, will it please you on your iourney for to walke.

Why Conditions, what Iourney thinke you, haue we to goe?

Nay let those that are louers iudge that, I say no mo.      **730**

I perceiue he will proue a foxe if you talke with him long,　Lam.
Who takes him foz any other, should proffer him much wrong. cla.

　Nay Mistres Clarisia if time conuenient would serue,　con.
I could proue that wemen comonly that name doth most deserue.
But if you please to depart, I redy am to waight.

　Come Lady, foz we intend from hence to wend straight.　Lam.
Proceed my deare foz Clarisia is prest to fulfill
Your minde in euery respect accozding to your will.
Wherfoze Conditions come and waite still on vs.　Exit

　Nay if I be behinde then hang me as hy as the house.　con.
Ha are they gone? was euer knaue beset in daine so befoze?
Affection quoth you? well fare at a pinche euermoze.
Foz if I had not roundly answered to my counterfeit name,
It would surely haue redownd to my vtter shame.
But howsoeuer the wozld goes parasites part I must play,
Foz to get my lyuing I can finde no other kinde of way.
Well I must after to the Dukes place, euen as fast as I may,
But in the end marke how the crafty knaues part I will play.

　¶Here enter Sabia alone.

Like as the Rat that once hath tast of Rosalgar oz bayne,　Sabia.
　Runnes presently to some moist place to cole her poisned pain:
So I being possest (alas) thzough Cupids dierfull dent,
Doth line in pyning state foz aye, that life is well ny spent,
Ha sweet Nomides who causer art of this my griefe and wo.
Foz Cupid he hath fozced me all pleasures to foz go,
In that vnegally at mee his poisoned shaft hath raught,
To cause me set my loue on him who wil set me at naught.
But foz his sake I fade as doth the flower in somners day,
I pine as doth the Merline shee that could not win her pzay.
I greeue I waile my lucklesse lot, I am in wofull state,
I finde no way that may impaire, oz this my sozrowes bate.
I curse may sure the time that I did vewe thy comly face,
I know right well in vaine it is to sewe to thee foz grace.
I perce the heauens with my dole, and lamentable cry,
I craue of blinde Cupido hee, my sute not to deny.
Why was it not my chance alas a princes foz to bee?
Why was my fortune to be bozne of base and low degree?
Why was it ah my destiny to be a Phisicions childe?

Why was it not my fortune ha,to come of stocke so milde.
Whereby I mought enioy thy loue ha worthy knight most stowt,
Whose comlines doth far surpas the knights of Phrygia rowt.
Which causeth me through feruencie to craue of thee thy loue,
Though womanhoode denayes the same,and doth me sore disproue
Well,here enters hæ him selfe alone , now helpe ye gods of might
And graunt that I obtaine my seute which I deserud by right,
But first I will go throud my selfe in corner secretly,
To heare if that for any one hæ will seeme to reply.
　　　　　¶Here enter Sir Nomides. 　　　　　(spoyle

omides. Though raging stormes of winters force hath done their worst to
　　　　Though Boreas w̄ his boisterous blasts doth range in every soyle,
　　　　Though clotted hard Accarnous frost doth fréese on dale and hill:
　　　　Yet can the warmed sotherne winde their raging forces kill.
　　　　Though fortune shæ did frowne on me,& wrought for me such fate
　　　　Yet at the last all stormes once past shee smiles on myne estate.
　　　　Though banisht I from cuntrey soyle and natiue kinsfolke deare,
　　　　Yet hath the powres assind to mee a knightly liuinge heare.
　　　　Wheras I leade my life at rest,where I minde to remaine,
　　　　Untill the sisters cut the thred of vitall life in twaine.
　　　　As for my vsuall name is tornd,and for euer will forsak,
　　　　And terme my self sir Nomides , a knight of lowe estate.
　　　　Wherby I quietly may rest,and liue at ease for aye.
　　　　But contrary if knowen I were,it would tourne to my decay.
　　　　But for to thinke of father mine,it grǽues my carefull brest,
　　　　That hæ should rainge in cuntreis strange,& I should liue at rest.
　　　　And eke farewell my sister deare,whom I haue left behinde,
　　　　In cruell tyrants murdering hand,thy life end for to finde.
　　　　I can not chewse but must acurse the time I fled away,
　　　　And left thée so behinde to rest vnto thy foes a pray.
　　　　I can not but must neds confesse I worthy am of shame,
　　　　In leauing thee a pray to those that sone thy death did frame.
　　　　A cruell brother,mought thou say I did remaine to thée,
　　　　That like a dastard fled away when I thy gard should bee.
　　　　Well in vaine it is for to repine , sith that the powers are bent
　　　　To woorke their fury on them twaine,I must be well content.
abia. 　　　　Well met Sir knight thus solitary in fields your selfe alone.

770
780
790
800

24

I am penſiue Lady but yet welcome to me as any one. Nomid

Not ſo ſir knight, I thinke you beare to Ladies no ſuch loue, Sabia.

My Lady how know you that, you did me neuer pzoue. Nomid

She ŷ ſhould pzoue I thinke ſhould finde in you ſum ſuttel gyle Sabia.

You weemen ſure are ful of ŷ though oftentimes you ſmile Nomid

We wemē? nay, in men you would ſay foz wemē mean to true Sabia.

Say you ſo Lady?foz experience then mark what woozds enſue. Nomid

Speake fozth your minde I am content if ſo you will not faine Sabia.

If ſo I do Lady, I doubt not, but you will reply againe. Nomid

And reaſon good if wzongfully you wemen would diſpzoue, Sabia.

Not wzongfully but rightfully I ſhall expzes your loue. Nomid

And therfoz Lady heare my talke that I in bzeef ſhall ſpeake,

And after if you pleaſe, againe reply your minde to bzeake.

Firſt what loue I pzay you bare Helena vnto her lozde and kinge?

What conſtancy in Creſeda did reſt in euery thinge?

What loue, I pzay you, beare Phedria vnto her Theſeus,

When in his abſence ſhe deſſered his ſonne Hippollitus?

What true loue eke bare Medea vnto Duke Iaſon hée?

Tuſh Lady in vaine it is to talke, they all deceitfull bée,

And therfoze lady you muſt yéeld to me in that reſpecte.

Men ſtill are iuſt though wemen muſt their plighted vows neclect

Muſt? why belike you thinke it comes to them by courſe of kinde Sabia.

Not I my ſelfe do ſay the ſame, but in auctoz I it finde. Nomid

In Auctoz then you haue an aid foz to diſpute with mée? Sabia.

But foz all your aid in way of ieſt againe I will reply,

If ſo you will atentiue bée to that I here ſhall ſpeake.

With willing hart I do agrée that you your minde ſhal bzeake. Nomid

Then ſir knight how faithfull was Eneas to Didoes grace? Sabia.

To whom he plighted faith by vowe none other to imbzace.

How faithfull was Duke Iaſon hée whom Medea did ayd?

When hee to win the goulden fléece by Otes was diſmaid?

And Theſeus I pzay you alſo how faithfull did hée bide

When that the bow he once had made to Ariadne he denide.

How faythfull was Deomedes one of the Greekiſhe crew

Though Troilus therin was iuſt yet was hée found vntrewe,

And ſo betwéene thoſe twaine, and foztunes luckles hap,

Shée was like Lazer faine to ſit and beg with diſh and clap.

D.                                              Tuſh

Tush tush you sée to trust to men whose fickle braines are so,
That at the first sight of euery wight their plighted vowes for go.
And therfore you must wey in minde, though wemen sometime
Men wil do so though to their wo it doth ensew I wisse.     (misse

_lomides._    In déede lady I must confesse that you the truth haue sayd,
Then say that you were conquered in talking with a mayd
_ibia._    Nay lady he that talkes with you vntill the field he gaine,
_lomides._    Should proue the labour he should take both frustrate, fond & vain
For why: though men can win in field both honour praise, & fame
Yée wemé by their suttel slights full soone their deaths can frame.
And therfore lady I must graunt you are to stronge for mée,
And if I were a iudge certeine ye wemen should Lawyers bée.
_ibia._    Wemen: why thé what would you haue poore witles mé to say

    850

_lomides._    To stand and heare, and iudge aright vpon the wemens play.
_ibia._    Wel then shal you be a iudge to that which I in place shal speak
_lomides._    Wel thé procéde & let mée heare what words you mean to break
_ibia._    There was a ship that chanst to sayle a thwart the raginge sea,
And being in the middest therof at anker and at ease:

    860

In sodden there arose a storme and silly barke so tost,
In such a raging kinde of sort, that Ankers all were lost.
Now Ankers being gone, and Cabels in like case:
The silly Barke by tumbling waues was tost from place to place.
The Mariners did quake for feare to sée that luckles day,
That to the gods with humble sute they all began to pray.
The gods then hearing of their plaint and lamentable cry:
Did driue them straight by force of winde vnto an hauen by.
Wheras they hope for aye to rest if powers do graunt them grace
Lo now sir knight iudge you aright on this my wished case.

    870

_omides._    Na Lady if you put so hard demaunds vnto your iudge at furst:
Yée must haue time to pause theron lest he should iudge at worst.
Then would you put some blame in him and say he did you wrong
Therfore he giues the iudgment to your selfe that are so stronge.
God Lady let me here thesame, I hartely require.
_ibia._    In hope to haue my wished will you shall haue your desire.
The Ship which I spake of before is I my selfe sir knight:
And being once inflamed alas, by Cupids raging flight.
Was tost on wayes of wrackfull wo, and all for thy swéete loue,

    I

I fozced was with humble sute to craue of gods aboue
To send to me some pleasant time that I with you mought talke,
Where now it was my chance sir knight to finde you in this walke
I fozced am of feruency to craue of you your loue
And eke to set all shame aside your god will foz to pzoue.
Graunt me therfoze, O wozthy knight that none but onely I,
Shall thée posses, foz louing sere, vntill we both shall dye.
Refuse me not that am thy friend who loues thée as her life,
And graunt that none but Sabia shalbe thy only wife.
Lo this is all O wozthy knight, that I of thée require,
Fozsake not thy deare ladies sute, but graunt to her desire.

    Madame the hart that once is fixt oz set and hath y likes him best *Nomid.*
What needs it foz to seeke foz moze tobzæde his moze vnrest?
My hart is fixt vpon the thinge that I all redy haue,
And therfoze Lady in vaine it is of mée such loue to craue.
I am none such that liues by loue, I serue not Venus traine,
I fozce not of blinde Cupid hée, I hould him in disdaine.
Though Poets terme him aged and say he shootes from skie,
The which by good experience I straight shall here deny.
Lust fauozing folly fond, did falsly fozge and faine
Loue foz a god, because he mought his frédome moze attaine,
And therfoze leaue of sute, and craue no loue of mée,
Whiles I haue life this is certaine I will no louer bée,
And therfoze lady now adue.     **Exit.**

    A wo be to the time that first I did begin to sewe,     *Sabia.*
Now fare well all my hope of him whom I thought to enioy,
Whose sight it was that fozced me to waile with great anoy,
Ah cruell gods of loue, O crafty cancred wight,
That wzekes thy fury vpon mée, and touchest not that knight.
Ah sir Nomides, whiles I do liue in ioy,
None other shall attaine my loue though it bzéede mine anoy.
And still will I incroche on thée, thy onely loue to haue,
Though foz thy sake I should betake my self to wofull graue. **Exit.**


    ¶Here entreth Conditions.
Ah ah ah this geare cottens I may say to you.     *Condi.*
    I haue wzought a fetch to set thé by y eares hap what shal ensue
                D ij                 By

By my honesty it doth me good that I so crafty should bée
For the Dutches is fallen out with Clarisia long of mée.
For I told certein of her waiting maides how ŷ people in ech place
Giues Clarisia the prayse and sayes shée excels the Dutches grace.
Which when she heard so chafed that it was straung to beholde, 920
On the other side Lamphedon would not haue his lady controwlde,
Thus haue I set them together by the eares hap what hap shall,
And marke the end of this geare which way it shall fall.
For Clarisia hauing to vnkle Mountaynio kinge of Thrace,
Will no longer here abide but straight waies thither will trace,
And now at the sea coast haue I bin shipping to prouide,
For my Master Lamphedon and Clarisia against the next tide.
I must away rome for a cutter that is euery ynche a man,
A villain that will set a thousand by the eares if hée can.

⟨Here entreth Lamphedon and Clarisia. 930

amphe. Clarisia and my deare wife before the gods by vow,
　　　With listinge eare do marke in briefe what I shall say to you,
Though mother mine the Dutches shée such rigor sémes to show,
And all for the good will which I to you do bear and owe:
Let not the same dismay your minde cast pensiuenes aside,
For till that life be tayne from mée my truth shall sure be tride.
And therfore Lady séme not to depart, I thinke it best.

a. A my Lamphedon deare leaue of, and graunt thy loues request
Sémé not to stay with lady thine in Phrygia to her wo,
But come and wend we presently, to Thracia let vs go. 940
For my vncle Mountanio kinge of Thrace, hath sent for mée,
And in his letter hée hath sent, my louing knight, for thée.
Desiryng vs to come to him, and that in continent,
For why hée hath no childe aliue, wée know not his intent,
Perchance, my deare, hée will bestow on vs some goods or welth,
Wheras we may more quiet liue in perfecte Ioy and health.
And so our absence may in time obtaine your mothers loue,
Wheras our presence being heare to anger doth her moue.
Wherfore my loue deny me not, but let vs hence depart.

amphe. A cruell mother to thy childe chéfe cause of this his smart. 950
Must I from lyked soyle depart on seas in ship to sayll
Where oftétimes through force of waues ŷ carued plācks do faill.

Must

Mult Lady mine talt the like wronge? a cruell parents sure.
That to your only sunne you could, sutch heapes of care procure.
¶Here entreth Condicions suddenly.

Gods ames, are you here I haue bin seekyng you all aboute,
To certifie you of newes whiche are so true out of doubt.
The duke your father hath made great searche for you twayne,
And doth intend to imprison you bothe, this is playne.
And all vpon the request of the Dutches if you do not flie
I am afrayde you and your Lady are like for to die.
And therfore of all loues come come let vs away.

Condicions, come hether man, and a whyle do thou stay,
I pray thee tell mee, is it true that thou dost now say?

What a mad man are you? take mee with a lye,
And whip mee that all villaynes may take example thereby.

Ah cruell parents to your childe, and would you seeke his death?
And can your harts agree in one, to stop his vitall breath?
Ah Heauens, shall man in crueltie passe the Lyon fearce in feild.
Which can compell eache liuing beast vnto his strength to yeelde?
Yet the Lyon doubts to slay his whelp, or do it any wronge.
The Serpent with the Tiger eke, whiche are both fierce & stronge
Will neuer seeme at any time their younglinges for to greeue,
But will them norish tenderly till they haue strength to liue.
Is nature cleane exiled quite from thee, my cruell Sier?
Is pittie put from out thy minde, to wreake on vs thy ire?
Is fatherly loue cleane gon from thee: is mercy not in minde?
Is crueltie crept into thee that thou art so vnkinde?
Ah Gods, now farewell Phrygia soyle, farewell ay parents twayne
Who seekes to put my loue and mee to death and cruell payne.
Ah my beloued Clarisia, I wayle to thinke of thee,
That ȳ shouldest sustaine sutche wronge for loue thou bearest mee.
Impute vnto thy louing knight no blame for this, my deere,
For gladly if I could, I would haue taried with thee heere.

Heere: then weare you vnwise if heere you would stay, tis plain
To haue your lady and your self of all holden in disdain.
And therfore without farther talke let vs abide no longer heere,
If you do I am afrayd you are like to bie your tarying deere.

Well then Conditions I pray thee w speed our shipping prepare.

Condi.

Lamph

Condit.

Lamph

Condi.

Lamph

D iij                                      Tush

**ondit.** Tush tush, this is alredy done let that be the least end of your care, 990
And therfore of all loues let vs be gone, least vnwares wée be tayn
Misteris Clarisia, of all loues perswade him to depart amayne.

**a.** Ah my Lamphedon, wende we hence incontinent with spéede
For why, to worke our finall end they fully haue decréede.
You néede not feare for want of ship, Conditions hath béen thare,
At the sea coast alredie sure our shippyng to prepare.
And therfore let vs hence depart, and that incontinent.

**amphe.** Well then let vs depart, my deare, sith that you are so bent.

**ondi.** Are they gone? Conditions? Nay double condicions is my name 1000
That for my owne aduantage suche dealynges can frame.
Nay, if wee come in courte agayne to serue a kynge
Hange mee if I giue not a thousand of them the slynge.
To Thracie quoth you? there could be no better iorney for mee,
Well I must begone, for I can neuer be well till I a ship bord bée.

### ¶ The Mariners within.

**Master.** Ha la how, boyes a baste, ther cast haulser a land.

**l. mate.** Uere vere, come no neare least wee ground on the sand.

**oteswain** Lanche out the Cocke boyes, and set the Master a shoare.

**oye.** The Cocke is lanshed, eache man to his oare.

**ondi.** Harke, here comes our Mariners to séeke for Lamphe & Cla. they 1010
Who I am sure by this time already a shipborde bee.

**Master.** A shoare, a shoare, eche man on the lande.

**l. mate.** Boy, come vp, and ground the Cocke on the sande.

**ondi.** Twentie pound to a peny they are Pyrats y lands heer aboute.
Ha, I am beset in sutche a sort that I cannot get in nor out.
There is no remedy but I must stand to my tackling hap good or il.
I must needs draw, but if I fight it shalbe agaynst my will.

### ¶ Here entreth the Pirates with a songe

**Master.** Ha coragious my mates, and excellent well done.

**l. mate.** By gogs bloud Master we weare happy when to rob we begun. 1020

**oteswain** It doth me good to see what booties we haue had on the seas,
Which redownes to our profit, though to others disease.

**oy.** Though I be but shipboy I must needs speake my minde
If the whole seas were searched, such a shipful of théeues you could

**All.** Speake soft goodman boy, least wee be espied.        (not finde.

What

What Pirats? Nay incontinent I will haue that tried.     Condi.
Gogs wounds defende ye,for yle take you all my selfe.
Wilt thou so?nay,none but the shipboy shal deale with the elfe.    Master.
With a boy? if you be men draw,and come trie with me all.    Condi.
Wilt thou so? by gogs bloud this is a bould enterprise of a squal   M.mate
Well sith he will needes,Ile deale with him my self hand to hãd   Boteswa
Come on then,strike it out at length:but what ar you mariners   Condi.
I will not deale then with you for all this land.
For they bee good fellowes,they be no quarelers.
Why not with Marriners I pray thee:come let vs try it out.    Boteswa
Stay thy hand,it shall not be so,to put thee out of dout.    Condi.
Were it to dry water souldiors I would deale if here were a skore
For I haue dealt with fortie at a time and more.
Then it were to mutche for me to deale with you alone.    Boteswa
That is true,for of a littell man where I hit I breake the bone.   Condi.
I pray you sir shew vs why you beare Mariners such good will?   Master.
Because I am a Mariner my self and haue excellent good skill.   Condi.
And haue you satch excellent good skill in deede,    Boteswa
Then why like a landeman go you in sutch a weede?
Lest the good deeds which I haue done on the seas    Condit.
Redowne to my small comfort and ease.
Why then it seemes by thy talke thou hast bin a Pirat or this?   Boteswa
Yea in faith haue I, and that knowes Mariners ships Iwis.   Condi.
By gogs bloud I will haue him a shipborde or els I will die.   Master.
That is enough Ile take you at your word seyng there is no re-   con.
Wil you haue me a shipbord whether I wil or no?     (medie,
Yea surely defende thee,for I intende so.    Master.
Stay,stay,shall I be a sharer if quietly I go with you aborde?   Condici.
There is our hands,wee will make thee our captayn at a word.    All.
A captayne:here is my hande,to go with you as is your desier.   Condi.
But it were vncomly to play the sea man in landemans attyer.
No more thou shalt,for our other Captayne is dead,    M.mate
And thou shalt haue his attyer,and his roome,and lie in his bed.
Well then come on and let vs a shipborde straight.    Condi.
Wee are all redy on our Captaine for to waight.    All.
But sirs,there is a bowtie towards if you follow my aduice   Condi.
And go to worke withall,and shew your selues wise.

                         What

All.     What is that,Captayne?declare to vs all.

Condi.     It is a pray that will euriche both great and small.
And tis this,there is a certayne Gentilman with a Lady,
Readie shipt to sayle into Thrace,
with great aboundance of riches and wealth.
Now if wee could get into their way by stelth,
Wee should haue sutch a boutie that wee neuer had sutch another.

Botefwain     By gogs bloud he is an excellent Captayn,& far excels our other     1070
Captayn let vs aboord,wee are bounde to do what you thinke best.

Condi.     Come on then,let vs away,& in Mariners attyer I were drest.
                              Exeunt.

¶Here entreth Mountagos with his daughter.

Mountag.     COme Sabia by and by and show your father straight and quéeke,
In what place in te body you be so sore séeke.
My tinke you haue te greta deseza in te belly and te heda.
By gots lorde Sabia you loue te man me am a frayda.
And you so do Sabia expresse to your father by and by,
By cotes lord me geue twenty hundret pounds in mariage truly.     1080
And terfore letta me kno te man good Sabia my childe,
For me kno wel experienza you loue te man me am no begilde.

Sabia.     Good Father seeme not to demaund the thing I cannot show,
The wyght whom bourdned I am with,of truth I do not know,
If that I weare in loue at all,in vayne it weare for mee
At any time to hide the same,sutch skill remaynes in yée.

Mountag.     A Sabia,say me nota so,for me kno by good experienza,
You loue te mana longe a go,terof a me lay a houndred penza.
Ha ha Sabia,how now,whata say you apon tis gea rea?
Me kno by good knoledga,and your countnance a deseza you beara     1090
And terfore Sabia expreza your fater whata Gentelman a bee,
Efata Sabia mee do whata mee can to maka te mariage truly.
If a be Marchanta,or Gentelmana,or knighta,or whata mana a be
Wit my passyng coninga,mee can make him loue tee.
And terfore expreza your satera by and by.

Sabia.     Wel sith there is no remedie in vayne it is to deny.
Syr Nomides it is that knight of Arabia,whom I do loue in hart,
And will vntill his loue I win,though I from life depart.
Lo now you know y wight,O Sier,whom cupid caused me to loue
                                            But

But by no meanes I can deuise, him will no pity moue.
Though oftentimes I did intreate, still casting shame a side,
As often he refused the same, and still my sute denyde.
Lo now my Sier, you know the wight whose sight hath perst my
That for his sake I may not take at all my quiet rest.        (brest

Sir Nomides, ha ha Sabia, data te mana dat causes you be seke so Monuta
Mee kno well you loue te man by good knolega longa go,
Well Sabia come home your faders house, mit out delay,
For me will go speake mit Sr Nomideza straight veay.
And me can mit my cunninga me will mary you twaine,
Terfore, Sabia, come home to your faters house me say againe.

Yes father sith that it is your will, I redy am to wayght.        Sabia
Well ten rom away, Sabia, mit your fater straight.   Exit Mounta.  Mounta
                                                                   Sabia
Ah cruell crabbed curish impe, ah stubborn strong stony hart,
That can constraine a lady so to suffer deoly smart.
How canst thou safely without shame denay a ladies proffer?
Perchance thou mayst liue thrise so long and neuer haue like offer
Ah heauenly powers do graunt that he may taste of my like paine
And graunt he fancy one whose loue he neuer shall attaine.
And furies all agree in one to broyle within her brest,
Whom he shall fansy in such sort that shee may him detest.
Then know I that he feeles my paine, then tasteth hee my greife,
Then hope I that in time he will of mee take some releife.
And that the same may come to pas Alecto perce her brest,
That amongst all she vewes with eye, she may him most detest.
So hope I that in time I shall perforce obtaine his loue,
Through cunning skill of father mine, and helpe of gods aboue.
                        ¶Here entreth Lamphedon lamentinge.
AH gods how haue I bin through Pirats force on seas surprest? Lamphe
    When that we thought most quietly from foes to sayle at rest.
How haue the gods bin changable, or mutabell in this case?
How haue I bin on tumblinge waues sore tost from place to place
How did those cruell Pirats they my corps cast into seas?
And yelded me to Neptunes waues to cary me where he please.
How rigorously delt they with mee and my Clarisia deare?
Who I know well with cruelty was drowned with mee there.
Ah ye powers, is Lady mine bereft of life, or do I but surmise?

                                C                        D3

33

Oz do I but imagine so, oz do I but deuise?
Deuise what nede I to deuise on that with eares I heard?
Then wzetch vnto thy eares of fozce thou must giue most regarde
Delt not they cruelly with thæ? then what cause had they to stay  1140
But wozke thy ladies finall end, as thou didest here them say?
How can the swelling waues enclose that tender cozps of thine?
How could the cruell god of seas so vew thy latest fine.
A Zepherus, would thou hadst clod my loue in thy swæte blast,
When Pirats sloung her ouerbourd, and on soft ground her cast.
Why was it not my chance, alas to end my dayes in flood?
Why did the powers assine to mæ to land in place so good?
Ha wzetch hast thou fozgot that lady thine in seas is dzound?
Dzaw fozth thy lingering blade with spæde, & giue thy self a woūd,  1150
Sith that her ioy was ioy to thæ, let her death be thine also,
And with this gozing blade of thine dsride this hart from wo.


¶Here entreth the Mariners with a songe.


Lustely, lustely, lustely, let vs sayle fozth,
The winde trim doth serue vs, it blowes at the nozth


All thinges wee haue ready and nothing wee want,
To furnish our ship that rideth hereby:
Uictals and weapons they be nothing skant,
Like wozthy mariners our selues wee will try,
Lustely lustely, &c.


Her slagges be new trimmed set slanting aloft,
Our ship foz swist swimming oh shee doth excell,
Wee feare no enemies, we haue escaped them oft,
Of all ships that swimneth shee bareth the bell.
Lustely, lustely, &c.


And here is a master excelleth in skill,
And our masters mate hee is not to seeke:

Agd

34

And here is a botefwaine will do his good will,
And here is a ſhip boy wee neuer had his leeke.
      Luſtely luſtely,&c.


If fortune then faile not, and our next viadge proue.
Wee will returne merely and make good cheere:
And hould all together as freends linkt in loue,
The cannes ſhalbe filled with wine ale and beere.
      Luſtely,luſtely,&c.


HAy liuely by gogs blond this booty was for our purpoſe fit,   Maſter.
  It doth me good to thinke how I whozld him ouer bozd yet.
  And it doth me good to heare the lady at euery woozd,   Boteſwa
Deſtrous not to whozle her louer ouer bozde.
But ſhæ might cry her fill,for ſhee was neuer the ſoner heard,
For I helpt to whozle him ouer bozd to her crying I toke no regard
Whē our captaine heard it hee was in a rage ẏ it was ſtrange to ſe
And out of hand would næds fight, and ſaid it was longe of mæ.
  Sæing our captaine is gon with the lady to Marofus Ile away,   Maſter.
Let vs make haſte a ſhipbozde,without longer delay.
  Content Maſter we intend to tary no longer here.   Boteſwa
  Nay ſtay you Impes of limbo lake, I waight your coming nere   Lampho
Ah wzetches who haue dzound my loue in flouds of cruell force,
Defend you ſtraight,for I do waight to wzeke it on your corſe.
Wherfoze, I ſay,defend you ſtraight,my force you ſure ſhall try,
  Ah wzetch,and art thou yet aliue?be ſure we will the not deny   Maſter.
Ah gods what chance is this that hæ ſhould ſwim to land?
I repent by gods I ſweare I tide him not foot and hand.
But well,ſith that thou ſkaped art from dzowning in this caſe,
Prepare thy ſelfe,either thou oz wæ ſhall end their liues in place,
Wherfoze ah wzetch wæ thæ defy as enemy to thy face.
  In hope of victory I of you in my ſwæt ladies caſe.   Lamph
And therfoze wzetches prepare you to dy.   Boteſwa
  They were but fooles that from thee would fly.   (his life
Ha gods,he ẏ doth truſt to much his ſtrength may chance to loſe   Thei fig
  O ſtay thy hãd cozagious knight,god news hereof thy wife   Boteſwa
               E y          My

**nphe.**

My wife: ha wretch & and thy mate haue drouð her corps in seas

**ster.**

Ha no sir knight that is not so rygor some what apease.

And I shall surely show you al.

**mphe.**

In hope to heare good newes of thée, I sure pardon thée shall.

Stand vp & let mée heare with spéede what thou canst here expresse

**ster.**

Well, sith there is no remedy the truth I shall confesse

Thy lady shée hath still her life, and arriued in Phrygia here,

But going to Marofus Ile to liue as captiue there,

For why, we sent our captaine now to sell hir if he might,

To one Cardolus, who doth kéepe that Ile by valiant fight. 1210

Whom when he hath, he doth enclose in mighty turret hye,

To se if any dares presume his force and strength to try.

And lest that he should séeme perforce to take her and not pay,

Wée sent our captaine who will try his strength both night & day,

Unles he haue what is his dewe, lo here, O worthy knight,

Uouchsafe to haue remorce of mée who haue exprest the right,

And graunt that I may now depart with this my life away.

**mphe.**

In hope thou hast exprest the truth I minde thee not to stay.

Well for this once I pardon thee, depart hence when thou please,

**after.**

Then lustily once more by gogs bloud to the seas. 1220

Why I thinke it be my desteny to be hanged or drownd,

I thinke neuer to dy in my bed for a hundred pound. Exit.

**mphe.**

Proceede Lamphedon coragiously Cardolus strength to try,

And either win thy loue perforce, or in his hands do dye.

Shall Lady thine thus liue a thrall to tyrant fierce of might?

Shall thy sweete Lady waile for wo in turret day and night?

No Lamphedon, let féetsteps thine be prest to Marofus to trade,

In hope for to subdew the wretch with this thy goring blade.

Let manly courage there be showne let valiant hart be tried,

Let not this profered challenge eke of the once be denyed. 1230

Shall my Lady liue his thrall? no Cardolus thinke not but I,

Though thou hast Herculus force thy might and strength will try.

Or if that Cerberus his might did rest in body thine,

I would not dout for ladies sake thy vytall dayes to fine.

Which dun, my ioyes would new increase wher sorowes yet berife

If that through helpe of mighty Marce I may obtaine my wife

¶Here entreth Clarisia and Condicions

36

Misteris clarisia cast of care,                                                    Condit

   For your Lord Lamphedon do not feare

He is in health though you thinke him to be drownd,

And there of I dare lay fiue hundred pound,

   Oh Conditions, on that condicion I thinke all trauell no paine, cla.

If thereby I mought win my Lamphedon againe.

But, ha allas, he is drownd I am sure.

   Lady Clarisia, leue of this talke, that your greifes doth procure. Condi.

If you will follow my counsell and cast of all this dout,

I will deuise a meanes to finde my Lord Lamphedon out.

   Yes Conditions I am content and do agrée to thy will,                Clarisia

   Then in one respecte you must needs my request herein fulfill. Condi.

And that is this, you must be come a seruant to a knight,

Who dwelleth here hard by, who Leostines hight.

And whilst you abide there, my self wil go search all about

Night and day, vntill I haue found my lord Lamphedon out,

And when I haue found him, doubt you not but that we twaine,

Will by a suttell meanes conuay you from thence againe,

How say you lady to my deuice, are you herein content.

   Yes Conditions, to thy counsell I could well consent,                Clarisia

If therby I mought obtaine my louing knight againe.

   Doubt you not that I will omit any kinde of paine.                       Condi.

Untill I haue found him either on sea or land,

Beleue me as I am an honest gentleman here is my hand.

But I must request one thinge more you must change your vsuall

Lest you being knowen all our woes would frame.          (name

And wheras your name is Clarisia, let it Metrea bee,

Which done, I doubt but your knight in good helth you shall sée.

   I warant thée my name is Metrea what soeuer they say.          Clarisia

   Well you must your selfe to the knights place take your way. Condi.

But besides, you must counterfit your progeny as you may,

Lest in vttering the same you worke your owne decay.

   Doubt you not Conditions for that I was borne in Phrygia here Clarisia

   That is sufficient, what soeuer they demaund, hould you there. Condi.

Well Lady here lies the ready way towards the knights place,

Depart when you please, I must seke out my master in any case.

   Content conditions, and farewell till we mete againe.            Clarisia ondit. You will not beléeue how I greeue at the partyng of vs twayn,

arisia. I pray thée be content Conditions, wayle nomore for mée.

ondi. Ha my good M. & my good Ms. for you I am as sory as I can be,

arisia, I pray thée leaue of Conditions, in hope of mery meetyng. Exit

ondi. Ha now a plague of al such vilains ὑ caused vs haue such gretig

Ha my good mistres leaue you of your wayling so sore for mee.

For I know you to wel, kinde harted for to bee.      (wherfore

What is she gone? haue I bin howling all this while & know not

Nay and she be gone so soone, by her leaue ile lament no more.      1280

Ah sira, to sée the dissimulation of a craftie counterfit knaue,

That by flatterie can brynge to pas the thinge he would haue.

Wept quoth you? I haue wept in deed to put you out of doubt,

Euen as mutch as wil driue halfe a dousen milles aboute.

But I must laugh to thinke on my Pirats filching knaues,

Their captayne hath boarde them through their noses like slaues.

They were not contented to make me captain to serue them abord      1290

But they must make a Marchant of me with target and sword,

Thinking I would deale with Cardolus if he would take her away

Nay by your leaue for weemens causes ill deale with no such play.

Fight whoso list, for mee.

But by this meanes I haue deuised to set the Lady free.

I would not be a borde agayne for fiue hundreth pounde,

I dare sweare in one hower I should be both hanged, kild, & drownd

well let me se whether shal I trace my Maister for to finde?

Let me see? welfare a head that can bryng sutch things in minde.      1300

It may be that he hath heard the Pirats for to say,

That they would send his Lady to Marofus Ile to sell her away.

And that he is gone thither to win hir from him agayne,

Here is no remedie I must thither, and that a mayne.      Exit.

¶Here entreth Lamphedon.

Lamphe. Though depe dispaire doth driue in doubt dew honor to disgrace.

Though dredful domps doth daunt ὑ minde being in vncoth place

Though hart is harded to hasard forth in ladies cause to try,

Against her cruell crabbed fo, and venture life to dy.

Yet must he be aduisedly, and in such kinde of sort,      1310

That as well through wit as strength it may deserue report.

Therfore Lamphedon take good hart like Troyelus in strength,

And

And I liue in hope through fearce affault to foyll thy fo at length,
Though that thou want Vlyſes ſkill foꝛ to imagin iuſt,
Oꝛ to deuice in righteſt wiſe which way begin thou muſt,
Beehold in hart through fearce aſſault thy cruell fo to foyle,
And end his days to merit pꝛayſe, oꝛ yæld thæ to the ſpoyle.
I ſtraight will ſammon on his ſhield to try his foꝛce and ſtrength,
In hope through helpe of mighty Marce to win the field at length
Thou Tirant Cardolus, who doſt incloſe within thy foꝛtres ſtrong
Faire ladies to their moꝛtal griefe, and pꝛoferſt them ſuch wꝛong.
Come foꝛth, foꝛ lo Mawger thy foꝛce Ile ſommon on thy ſhield,
In hope to ſet thoſe Ladies fræ, and end thy dayes in fielde.

¶Here entreth Cardolus.

What vaunting varlet dares pꝛeſume to try cardolus ſtrength?
  Who neuer delt w none as yet, but foyled them all at length?
Who dares a liue pꝛeſume to tread within Marofus Ile,
Except hæ lycence craue of mee: Ile cauſe him ſtraight requyle.
What wight aliue dares once pꝛeſume to ſomon on my ſhielde?
Who dares pꝛeſume foꝛ ladies cauſe to try my ſtrength in field?
And yet my thought I heard ſome one to ſomon on the ſame,
Tyſh cardolus, he is fled foꝛ dꝛede and hides his hed foꝛ ſhame,
  No cardolus, thinke not but I who pꝛeſent here do ſtand,
Dare try thy ſtrength with coꝛage bould, & foyle thæ hand to hand,
What thinkeſt thou that I come to thæ, to ſomon on thy ſhielde,
And dare not vew thy warlike ſhowe, that thou doſt make in field?
Yes yes cardolus pꝛepare thy ſelfe, if ſo thou thinkeſt beſt,
Foꝛ lo to ſet thoſe ladies fræ behould I here am pꝛeſt,
And therfoꝛe yæld them ſtraight to me from out thy pꝛiſon ſtroug,
Oꝛ els pꝛepare, to try thy ſtrength I will no time pꝛolong.
  Alas poꝛe wꝛetch, what meaneſt thou to trace from natiue ſoyle
To end thy daies, by me thy fo within Marofus Ile?
Thinkeſt ẏ thy ſelfe mæſt matched, wꝛetch, to deale in fight w mæ
In faith pꝛincor, I doubt not but ſoue thy courage colde ſhalt bæ.
  What cardolus firſt let vs try, and when that wee haue done,
Let him that doth ſubdew his fo vaunt of the victoꝛy wone,
Foꝛ why, the wight that reckeneth befoꝛe that hæ obtaine,
May chance to reeken twice, and then his reckning is in vaine.
So thou to vaunt of victoꝛy befoꝛe thou gaine the ſame,

1320
1330
1340

Cardolu
Lamph
Cardolu
Lamphe

Mayſt

Watt chaunce to haue thy Pecoks tail brought low vnto thy shame
And therfore let vs first begin,and when that wée haue doone,
Let him triumphe with victorie that hath the conquest woone.

ardolus.     Datst thou me so prinkor,with spéd then defend thée.
mphe,     Do thy worst Cardolus J feare not so J intend mée.
ardolus,     O gods,for want of breath my might beginnes to fayle.
mphe.     Then Lustily Lamphedon thy fo to assayle.   (grace
ardolus,     O stay sir knight,end not through fight my daies, but graunt me
amphe,     A wretch J denay thée,for J intend to stay thée or J frō hence trace.
ardolu.     O stay thy hand most worthy knight,and grant to me my life,
And thou shalt sée if in my hould there do remaine thy wife.
amphe.     Nay wretch that shall me not suffice,for J will straight set frée
All ladies,that within thy hould as it remaining bée.
And yet besides Ile end thy daies or J from hence do go.
Cardolus.     O stay thy hand most worthy knight,and worke not my last wo,
All that which apertaynes to mée J fully yeld to thée,
If so thou wilt ostend thy grace,and pardon graunt to mee.
Lamphe,     Well, J am perswaded in my minde thy pardon for to graunt,
All though at first or we begone of victory thou didst vaunt,
Yet shall it be to this entent,thou yéerely shalt resine
For this Marofus Ile the which J may now kéepe as mine
Fyue hundred crownes yerely to pay at penticost the same,
Or else be sure the sum vnpayd,Ile end thy dayes with shame,
And eke besides ile set them frée that in thy hould do rest.
How sayst thou now,do answere mée as please thy fansy best.
Cardolus.     O worthy knight J graunt thereto the tribute for to pay,
And liue thy thrall at becke and call vntill my dying day.
And eke beside those ladies which thou camst for to set frée.
Take here the keys with humble hart J yéeld them all to thée.
Lamphe,     Well then stand vp, cardolus, straight and let vs hence depart,
For who to vew my lady she J do desier with hart.
Wherfore Cardolus come away J charge thée straight with spéd,
Cardolus.     J redy am to waight Sir knight when you shall thinke it néede.
    ¶Here entreth Nomides.
Nomides.     AY gods,what wight hath greater cause for to lament then J,
That caused am to craue the thing that oft J did deny?
What wight would sew vnto his to whom oft he did offend?

D2

1350

1360

1370

1380

40

Oz mercy craue at any time of cruell crabbed frend?
Ha Nomides thou fozsed art to bow to Cupid hee,
Whom thou befoze didst so abhoz his captiue thzall to bee.
Why did I spight like retchles knight thy cunning state ozfozce?
1390   Why did I eke this defame speake, iust cause of no remozce.
Ha gods, am I become a louer now, oz sewter foz to bee,
Whom earst did fozce no whit foz loue, noz foz Cupido hee?
Would gods when first I bewed the sight of Metrea that dame,
Whose cumly fauour it was that fozste my hart to flame,
I had bin bewing of the thing which man doth most detest,
Then should not wofull louers paines haue bzoyled in my bzest.
Ha Metrea, wolde gods my soze were in thy bzest a griefe,
Then would I nothing doubt but that in time to haue releefe.
Why Nomides, doost thou not know shee is but a seruant shee?
1400   And thou a knight, and baliant wight of famous stocke to bee.
Why shouldest ý ought dispayze herein, but boulden fozth my hart
Sith that thou art constrained thzough fozce of blinde Cupidos dart
But ha alas, this greeues my hart that Leostines her Master hee,
Of longe hath bin foz fozmer grudge an enemy to mee.
Which will bee cause I may not come to speake with her at all,
Poz bew her crystall hew whose sight it was that fozst my fall.
But stay, good newes, I see here enters thy Ladies woman foole,
Whom shee foz charity toke in, and kepeth yet to schoole.
Now shall I know of simple soule where my sweete Lady is,
1410   Oz send her letter if I please, and of her sight not misse.

¶Here entreth Lomia the naturall.

HEy delading delading dats a good boy,             Lomia.
   Thou shalt go with me a sonday.
Ha barlaking I am a trim scholler, and a good wench indeede,
My lady sayes and I will learne well and take heede,
Shee will giue me a trim beluet cap with a fether,
To put on my head against colde weather.
And my lady will make me a trim longe cote downe to the ground
And if any wil mary mee, shee wil giue him twenty & a hūdzed poūd
1420   My lady can dance, so shee can and I must learne to,
Else I shall neuer get me a husband, foz all that euer I can do,
And my Lady can play tedull tedul in a paire of virgine holes.
                        F                And

And I must learne euery day,to as soone as I haue set in coles.
My Lady wilbe heare anone,and we must walke togethr,
If it hould vp and do not raine but be faire weather.
Dats a good baby cry out than.
And thou shalt haue a napell a nan.

  Now hope doth say I shall obtaine the sight of Lady deare,
If for her sake some paynes I take to stay her comming heare.
Ile fall in talke with this her foole till shee aproche in place,     1430
Wherby I may more familierly declare to her my case.
How now faire lady,whether pas you this way?

_omides._

_omia._   For sooth my lady her none selfe did?

_omides._   What did thy lady?

_omia._   Mary giue me leaue to go play.

_omides._   Who is thy lady and what is thy name?

_omia._   I am Lomia and she my Lady Metrea that late hither came.

_omides._   How sayst thou,my Lady Lomia,wilt thou change cotes wt mee?     1440

_omia._   No thinke not you haue a foole in hand I waraunt yee.

_omides._   Why Lomia,my cloke will become thee excellent and braue,

_omia._   Away Ile none of your clokes Ile tell my lady you are a knaue.
I can not on my ladies arant go,
But you wilbe medling with maids whether they will or no.
If thou werst no honester then I thou wouldst play the knaue,
But Ile tell my lady on thee so I will what thou wouldest haue.

_omides._   Nay Lomia do not and Ile giue thee a peny to by thy baby clouts.

_omia._   A you mocke so you do,you do but flowts.
Gafer a you mocke,yowill giue vs none at all,

_omides._   Here it is Lomia to by thee a Minefur cap or a calt.

_omia._   O god,is it good to eate gafar,how say you?     1450

_omides._   Taste it Lomia,tis some hard to disgest I tell yon trew.

_omia._   O god, O god Ile tell my Lady shee will be here by and by,
That you giue fokes hard geare to eat to make them cry.
O god my Lady come to this hangman,
And beat him away.

    ¶ Here entreth Metrea.

_etrea._ HOw now my Lady Lomia,how chance it you do stay?

_omia._   My Lady heres a hangman wil not let maides alone,
But giues fokes hard geare to eat as hard as a bone, (with a knife
Did he Lomia we wil put water in his poraige & cut his rost meat     1460

42

But perchance he is inamozed of thee, hée will haue the to his wife

   Ile be none of his wife my lady he is a trim husband foz you,   Lomia.

   I perceue though foeles want discression yet their meaning are Nomide

Faire lady in absence yours as I abzoade did trace,     (trew

I met your femall foole, with whom I had conferrance foz a space.

Df which I hope you will accept the same in way of Iest.

And not to iudge of simple men as wemen thinke it best.

   Though wemen some there be that iudge of men deuoyd of skil Metrea.

Ther are sure thzice as many men that deme of wemen yll.

And therfoze sure that argues not, men do the wozst they can,

And wemen, by your leaue, at times will do as yll as man.

   What tho, Syz knight, lets leaue this talke I am no pleader I, Metrea.

   Yet hear my talke, D perles dame, and then seme to reply, Nomide

   At your request a while Ile stay, your talke sir knight to heare. Metrea.

   Thé hope I that nought but trew faith in mé shal wel appere. Nomide

Lady, ŷ woūded deare whose tender bzest is pzest to quarrel groūd

And fozced eke thzough fierce assaulte to yéld to rauening hound,

Foz spilling bloud to issue out from tender bzest apace,

Beginnes to trudge with tripell steps befoze his foes in chase,

The egar hound pursues a maine till dear his some doth cast

In midst of way, which plaine doth show he nere hath run his last,

The hound whose nature is to know what state the dear is in,

Foz to pzocure moze fresh assault he straight doth there begin.

And at the length he pulles him downe, except he water take,

which if he may, then is he sure the houndes will him fozsake.

So I whose hart is clouen in twaine thzough quarell fercely shot,

That from my tender bzest the blood like fountaines dzoppeth hot,

Am faine like deare thzough greedy hound from hozd foz to depart

By reason of the blinded boy that did me so subuert,

The hounds of griefe vnherdid me, and ozowned me in chace,

Where I with tripell steppes did flye, but they persued a pace,

Till at the length my strength did waste and running eke did faile

Foz why, the hounds of deepe dispaire my sensis did so assaile.

The froth also is redy cast vpon my tender backe,

Foz why, alas they me persued, but I being to slacke.

Now want I nought but water bzooke, which if I may obtaine,

D Lady deare then am I sure from hounds to scape vnslayne,

F ij                Lo

Lo heare deare dame, iudge of the same as lightly as you may.

etrea.       I shall sir knight vnto my might and simple skill here say,
A cursed may that Bioke be sure that would not you imbiace,
Foi whose sweet sake you wounded were, and eke pursued in chase
Her siluer streames, vnwoithy is her wounted course to keepe,
And foi sutche an enuious offence a thousand woes to reepe,
But if I weare the Bioke, sir knight, and that it lay in mee,
To ayde you from your cruell foes, and from this miserie,
I would. Wherfoie accept sir knight my good wil! if you please.

omides.       Fayie Lady, in none but you it lieth my soiowes foi to ease.
Tis you your selfe, O noble dame, whom you accused thus,
Who neuer knew my greif befoie, the truthe foi to discus.
You are the streames foi whose sweete sake I haue desired so,
After my greuious wounde once giuen to skape to, from my fo.
Accept, my sute, O pereles dame, denay not my good will,
But yeeld to me my wished piay which I desired still.
And let me not foi your sweet sake, O Lady, dye foi loue.

etrea.       Sir knight, there stay, demaund the thinge no moie y wil not
I am al redy linkt in loue with one who faithfull is.    pious
Foi whose sweet sake Ile neuer loue if of his loue I mis.

omides.       Why Lady, then you kill my hart foi aye.

etrea.       What nay: take a man to play such a part & the night shalbe day
Come Loinia, let vs hence straight wende.

omides.       Why Lady : then my life shall ende.

letrea.       No no sir knight, you neede not feare.

omides.       Well Lady, foi your sweet sake, the greifs I beare.

letrea.       Come, rise Loinia, and let vs hence away.      Exit.

omia.       Yes foisoth my Lady, shall wee go play?
Gafar I thanke you foi my peny to by my baby some cloutes,
O God, hanginan you, I foigot to tell that you did sloutes.   Exit.

omides.       O gods, how like is this the suet of Lady Sabia shee,
Who seekes eche way both night and day to gayn the loue of mee?
Now may I say that heauenly powers doth iustly me reward,
Foi that to Sabias piofered loue I toke so light regard.
Yet shall not this dismay me ought, yet once moie will I woe,
Experience showes faint harted knights wins neuer fayie ladies
And weemen are of nature such, they alwayes do requier,   (loue
         That

1500

1510

1520

1530

That men should sæke and also cræp to gayne that they desier.
                ¶Here entreth Lamphedon.

O Gods, what wight is pincht with payne as is Lamphedon hæ.    Lamphe
  what hart hath had so sodaine ioy and straight such miserie?
Clarisia for thy sake I forced nought to trie Cardolus strength,
In hope for to haue founde thæ there to bred my ioy at length.
But ha alas hope fayles mee now, experience plaine doth tell,
That cruell Pirats drownd my loue, in fsming waues that swel.
In vaine I did the combat fight with stout Cardolus hæ,
Would gods it had now bin his chaunce in fight to haue slaine mæ
Not Tantalus in hell doth fæle the torments which I taste,
Nor Sisiphus who rowles the stone, and it rebounds in haste.
Not all the Furies in like case, nor Impes of Limbo lake,
Scars fæls the torments I sustayne for my deare Ladies sake.
Wel Lamphedō sith Lady thine is dead, & drowned long time since,
Prepare to ende thy vitall dayes or thou depart from hence.
Draw forth thy blade, sæke to inuade, the breath that lies in breast
Regard not life, since care and strife will neuer let thee rest.
But first ye Muses nine refraine from notes of wonted ioy,
And from your instruments so swæt to wayle my great anoy.
Now seace thy playnts Lamphedon wretch, & end thy cares & wo,
And rid thy life with goryng knife or thou from Ile dost go.
And powers do graunt for to receaue my soule to heauens hie,
And that it there may take rest wher my swæt Lady doth lie.
                ¶Here entreth Conditions.

S Tay thy hand Cardolus, for I come not for to fight,        Condi.
  As I am an honest Gentilman, and a right courteous knight.
      Ha Gods, good newes I hope, for this the captain sure should be.
With whom they say they sent my loue to sell to Cardolus hæ.   Lamphe
Come forth y wretche and straight confesse wher my deare lady is
Or els to worke thy finall end, be sure I shall not mis.
      Ha Cardolus, I minde not fight to gayne fiue hundered pound.  Condit.
      Then wherfore didst thou venter to tread on his grounde?  Lamphe.
      Ha, to bring you such newes as is for your case.        Condi.
      What is that, expresse it quickly and sæme not to lease.  Lamphe
      If you take me with a lie, hange me like a counterfeit knaue.  Condi.
      Come forth, if it be for my behowfe, dew pardon thou shalt haue.  Lamphe.
                        F iii                          Ha,

45

| | |
|---|---|
| Condi. | Ha, was there euer villaine in suche kinde of takyng as I, |
| | I am so beset that tis vnpossible to deuise a lie, |
| | And shall please you Cardolus there is a certayne knight, |
| | Commyng to win away one of your Ladies fayre by fight. |
| | Now, I for good will I beare you came to tell you the same, |
| | Least in suddaine at vnwares your woes he should chance to frame |
| | For he is the veriest sot that euer lookt champion on the face, |
| | I dare sweare if you giue him a blowe he would run hence a pace. |
| Lamphe. | If all this be true, I thanke thee for thy good will, |
| | But I pray thee expresse his name that mindeth me such ill. |
| Condi. | Ah now am I readie to beray my self for feare. |
| | For I am in doubt that Lamphedon already hath bin heare. |
| | Well whither he hath or not, the truth needes I must say, |
| | Least I bæyng proued contrarie, should worke my owne decay: |
| | Ha and shall please you, Lamphedon is his name. |
| | The dukes sunne of Phrygia, that pretendeth the same. |
| Lamphe. | Ha wretche where is my Lady thou broughts to sel to Card, hee |
| | Confesse the trouthe, or be thou sure thy dayes soone ended shalbe. |
| Condi. | Ha Cardolus, stay thy hand, ile fight for no Lady I. |
| Lamphe. | No wretche my name is Lamphedon & that thou soone shalt trie |
| Condi. | Iesus know you not me, I am Conditions your man, |
| | And for naught els but to sæke you only I hither ran. |
| Lamphe. | Conditions stand vp, I haue subdued Cardolus & am neuer ȳ near |
| | And haue set all his captiues free but Clarisia is not theare, |
| | Whiche bræedeth my care, and impaireth my wealth. |
| Condi. | Be of good cheare, noble Lamphedon, your Lady is in health. |
| | But is in Phrygia as a seruant with Leostines hee, |
| | And liueth in great greif and miserie. |
| | For why, she thinks you not aliue but drownd this is plaine. |
| Lamphe. | Ha Gods is this true Conditions, and dost thou not faine? |
| Condit. | Iesus, why when did you take me with a lie? |
| | Be bould, that which I once say, I will not denis. |
| Lamphe. | How came my Lady to be a seruant I pray thee expresse |
| Cond. | As wee trace on our way the whole to you I shall confesse. |
| | But where is Cardolus, noble knight, that he is not in place? |
| Lam. | I haue pardoned him, conditions, and graunted him grace, |
| | Upon condition he shall neuer offend lady agayne, |

And

And eke to yeld me tribute whilst life hee doth retaine.
Well then let vs be Ioging towards your lady apace, — Condi.
That is the place to which I most desier for to trace. — Lamphe.
Wherfore with speede,condicions,come let vs away, — Exit.
Proceede on for by your leaue I minde not here to stay. — Condi.
I would it had bin my chance to trie with Cardolus hee.
Ha tis a wonder that sutch strength in a litle mans arme should be
But by your leaue tis good to be mery and wise the truth to say,
Tis not for the weake hart with the Lion for to play.
Wel there is no remedie, I must after my master Lamphedon hee,
For I dare swear hee thinkes it longe till with his Lady hee bee,
¶ Here entreth Leostines with Metrea.

Lady Metrea,and seruant eke,attentiue be with speede. — Leostines
For why to rest thy faithfull freind beholde I haue decreede.
Sith that the powers haue lent to me none heyre for to enioy
My Lordship great when sisters three shall breede my last anoy,
And sith in sutch strange kinde of sort thou hapnedst to mee.
Thou shalt from this time forth,deare dame,no more a seruant be
But I will take thee as my owne,and only daughter deare,
For that I se virginitie in thee doth still appeare.
And when that death shall end my daies,& I to ground am throwne
For vertues that in you wee se receaue euen as thine owne
My landes and lordships euery deal,but if the powers graunt life,
Wee will do what there lieth in vs,to spouse thee as a wife
Unto some knight of famous stocke,and so prefer thy state,
In matchyng thee with sutch a one,as shall thee not forsake.
Lo here deare dame accept mee still euen as thy only sier,
And when ỹ wants,aske what thou wilt,thou shalt haue thy desier
Right louing lorde Leostines,and only master eke, — Metrea.
Whose hart is set and also bent my only ioyes to seeke:
Do graunt your simple seruant here to vtter forth her minde,
And then accept her as she is,and as you do her finde. — Leostines
Why Metrea,aske what thou wilt,I am contented I. — Metrea.
Then ayde Appollo pleasant Muse mee rightly to reply.
Right reuerend lorde Leostines,and Master in like case,
I yeld your highnesse intire thankes,and if the gods graunt grace,
I shall your simple foundling,here still dewtifull remaine,
Else the heauens me consume with speede,& end my daies w paine

47

I am your simpell seruant here, and still would gladly rest,
But that your highnes hath deuisd what for my state is best.
Yet haue I one thing to demaund, O worthy lorde, of thée,
Which if I may obtaine, I doubt in happy state to bée.

Leostines.    Why what is that my Metrea? do straight expresse the same,
Metrea.    Tis all my whole desier, deare Lorde, to gaine a virgins name.
Leostines.    Why Metrea, what should you so desier to liue in such a solum
And through your singel life in time, to gain some mis report? (sort
Why should you eke disdaine the state of wedlocke in this case?
Or seeme for to abuse the law of Iunos noble grace?
No do not so, my Metrea deare sith that dame nature shée,
Hath framed with skilfull workmanship such cumlines in thée.
Thou mayst in time obtaine some one vnto thy louing féere,
As will thée count his chiefest Ioy, and onely darling déere.
Wherfore be reuld, perswade thy minde, incline to my request,
And I will séeke, if god permit, what for thy state is best.
Which shalbe also to thy minde, if so thou wilt agrée.

Metrea.    Ye heauens still do strengthen mée.
Deare lord Leostines, more to say my tounge vnable is,
To render you the entire thankes that you deserue I wis.
Yet hope I that your honnor will consider as you finde,
Sith that my tounge vnable is to vtter as I minde.
So graunt your simple seruant here to liue in Dians chase,
For so shée sets her whole delight eche folly to displace.
Shee forceth nought of Iunos games, shee countes them but abuse,
To rest in true virginity such games she will refuse.
Lo here, deare lorde, do graunt to her in virgins state to rest,
For why I thinke and deme in minde that for my state is best.
And not for that I thinke my wit should pas your noble skill,
But from my infancy till now haue I request it still.
Lo heere, déere lord, on knées I craue the somme of my desier.

Leostines.    Stand vp Metrea, sith thou wilt néeds, thou shalt the same aspier
I am content that thou shalt liue in virgines sacred law,
So that with out my full consent from thence thou neuer draw.
No this is all I binde thée to, answere mée I craue.

Metrea.    Do more I will not, noble lord, more then I all redy haue,
Leostines.    Well then come on let vs depart with spéede to court againe.

To

48

To wayght vpon your noble state I will omit no paine.    Metrea
O gods shall loue of gods constraine mee now my knight forsake?
Or flattering woords alure me once my wonted loue to slake?
Shall profered courtesie constraine mee, or moue my setled minde,
That at my louing lords returne he falsly should me finde,
No no Lamphedon, for thy sweet sake Ile euer faithfull rest,
Though they should seeme wt goring blade to perce my tender brest

But wo be to thy parents those that did vs so disseas,   Enter
And caused vs to fly from them for dread, vnto the seas.   Condi.
Wo be vnto those Pirates they, that did with cruell hand,
Euen drowne my loue before my face except hee swom to land.
Wo be vnto that cruell king euen of Arabia soyle,
Whose cruelty was chefest cause we vndertooke this toyle.
And last of all, wo bee vnto condicions that wretch,
Who left me here vnto my grief by suttell crafty fetch.
Now am I sure my Lord is dround though he did beare in hand,
When Pirats flong him out of ship through force he swam to land
Now am I sure he did but faine, to leaue mee here behinde,
When that hee sayd he would a broade my louing Lord to finde.
A cruell crafty peuish elfe, ha flattering fained frende,
That through thy fayned forged talke deceuedst me in the end.

  Iesus Madame why make such lamentation for the losse of mee  Condi.
  Ha, I am as the Turkel hath lost her make & more if worse may  Metrea.
  Why Lady, you haue no such cause for to complaine.   (bee  Condi.
  Yes conditions, for all that thou saidst I see thou doost but faine.  Metrea.
  Nay lady that shall you proue contrary your selfe by and by,  Cond.
Lamphedon come forth in continent to disproue a lye.

   ¶Here entreth Lamphedon imbracing his Lady.

L Amphedon? ha gods, thrice welcome vnto mee.   Metrea.
  And thrice as welcome, noble dame, vnto Lamphedon hee,  Lamphe
Who long hath wayld with pensiuenes the want of thee, my deare,
But now he doth reioyce in hart that he hath found thee heare.
Ha my deare Lady for thy sake I hazard did my life.
And did subdew Cardolus hee with battering blowes so ryfe.
In hope for to haue founde thee there, but seinge it was in vaine,
I sought most desperatly to end my daies with cruell paine.
But ha, I haue to yeld the powers most entire thankes & prayse,

                           G              iij

In that they sent conditions hée, else had I finde my dayes.
As I in time, most constant dame, the whole shall show to thée,
And partly I perceiue, my deare, thy constancy towards mée.
The which through fame is blasd abroad vnto thy lasting praise,
And shall in bookes regestered be when death shall finde thy dayes.
Lo to thy fame most constant dame report hath blased this.

*trea.*    And to thy prayse thy name to rayse report will neuer misse.
But, ha Condicions, pardon graunt and mercy eke offend,
For blaming thée without a cause who neuer did offend.

*ndi.*    Pardon? how can you aske pardon and do him such offence?
Bée your leaue roome therfore, I must néeds hence.     1730

*mphe.*    Nay Condicions stay and pardon my Lady if shée did offend,
And be sure for thy courtesy I will reward thee in the end.

*ndi.*    I haue bin a cutter amongst wemen though now at the last cast,
Well Madame through intreatie my anger now is past.

¶Here entreth Lomia for hir misteris and the vice iustling hir.
*mia.*    O God this littell hangman is iustling maides against the wall?
For if I had not stand stiffe to I had catcht a great fall.     1740
*ndi.*    Whom haue we hear margery milke ducke, or flower of y frying
Or Ione of the Iakes house, or misteris Marian?     (pan
Shée hath a face like a howlet and when shée begins to frowne,
There are no more wrinkels in her forhed thē in y backe of a gowne.
*mia.*    Madam this same hangman is lusty & can not let one be in rest.
Let mée a lone, Ile tell my Lady so you were best.
My lady, my lorde Leostler praise you come to him straight,
*trea.*    Stay a while, Lomia, and a non en his honour I will waight.
My lorde Lamphedon, come and wend we hence to court our way,
Where we do minde most secretly your person to connay.
Into our chamber, where we will awhile our selues retreat,     1750
And then vpon your luckles chance we minde for to debate,
And so in time connay our selues through priuy fetch away,
For why to liue in seruitude I sure ne will, nor may.
*mphe.*    Ha constant dame vnto thy frénd, whose pére is not aliue,
That to gaine thy frend his company such pleasāt featch canst oriue.
I sure am now constrained through force for to account thee wise,
*trea.*    Nay, my loue, not I, for it was Condicions deuise.

                                   Condicions

Condicions: ha gods, sure in such matters thou doost passe,   Lamph
Know you not how $y^e$ in wemens matters I am wisest $y^t$ euer was  Condi.
   Sure so thou art, but lady we must about it secretly,   Lamph
Lest some belonging to your lorde our dealings chance to spy,
which might through their impoysened hate procure our care, and
And so our secreats be disclosd, oz we from hence do go.   (two
   I warrant you my lord, you neede not so to feare.   Metrea.
   Well lady let vs go foz I desier foz to be there.   Lamphe
Condicions stay thou heare a while vntill we do retier.   Exit.
 Gods sames is it euen so wel, dispatch gentleman I hartely desier Condi.
Ha ha this geare cottons, now if her master Leostines hæ,
Knew that Lamphedon in lady Metreas chamber should bæ,
There were all the sport and pastime that should excell,
  Gods efaith I care not, foz I woull tell.   Lomia.
  Gods sames, Lomia, what wilt thou tell, and of what?   Condi.
  Of my lady, and of the trim gentleman, and thou goodman squat Lomia.
  Why Lomia, what didst thou sée mée do, I pray thée declare?  Condit.
  No no, Ile tell my lozde, so I will, I do not care.   Lomia.
  Then will I thrust my dagger in thy belly by and by,   Cond.
  O god I will not tell and you will not make mée cry.   Lomia.
  Then what wilt thou say when thou commest to Leostines hæ? Condi.
  Foz sooth Ile say twas not you that kist my lady, twas hæ.  Lomia.
  Gods sames wilt thou so, let me heare thée say so if thou dare, Condi.
  No I wonnot say so, Ile say my lady did not spare.   Lomia.
But kist you both first and then you kist her againe,
When I come there I will not tel of you twaine.
  wilt thou? then will I kill thée, and that out of hand,   Condi.
  I won not say my lady lead a man to her chamber by the hand. Lomia.
  In faith this geare is at a mad kinde of stay,   Condi.
Ha that I were able to fly from hence away.
The foole will vtter all to Leostines that shee hath heard oz séene,
Alas Lamphedon thou wildst wish this day had neuer béene.
Gods sames, I wolde I were hanged on some gebit that is stronge
     Here entreth Leostines with a lozde oz two moze,
My lozde I maruell why Metrea, absents her selfe so long?  Leostine.
   It séemeth that shee wayeth no whit our counsel geuen of late,
That thus her wonted courtesie shee séemes foz to abate,

                  G ij                   It

les.     It may be so, O worthy Lorde, as you haue heare exprest.
stines.  My Lorde attend me, I may not rest till truth shalbe confest.
ia.      My Lorde you wone not se my bord, you loke another waye.
stines.  What Lomia are you heare? how chanceth it you do staye,
         And bryng mee no more word from your misteris agayne?
nia.     Why forsooth, my Lord, I thought mutch to take so mutch pain
stines.  Where is thy Misteris, Lomia, that wee cannot her see?
nia.     Il tell my Lorde on you now, because you did beate mee.
         My Lorde, I wonnot tel my Lorde and yo will put vp your thinge.
stines.  What, is there any that would seeme to stynge,
         Or profer the foole any kinde of wronge?
ds.      It is but the fooles fashions, noble Lorde, the time to prolonge,
mia.     My Lorde, I did se nobody kis my Lady, so I did not law.
stines.  I see the foole hath hard & seen some thing that she standeth in aw
mia.     My Lord, my Lady is not gon to her chäber w a gentilman shee.
stines.  My Lords how like you this, it seemes she hath oft disceyued mee
mia.     Of trouth, deare lorde Leostines, wee needs must deem it so.
stines.  If this proue true, let them be sure, that I will worke their wo
mia.     No forsooth my Lorde, my Lady did not say so, forsooth twas bee
stines.  Why? what did he say?
mia.     Mary giue you poison to drincke, and cary my Lady away.
         Law, I did not tell of you, will you beat mee any more.
ndi.     Gogs wounds, out of my sight you crooked nose whore,
         By his wounds what shift shall I make to skape away from hence
         I stand in such a quandary that I would giue my life for two pece.
         Let me alone, it is good to saue one, as far as I can see,
         I will step in and affirme the fooles talke most true to bee.
         So if the worst fall I shall be sure my selfe for to saue cleare,
         Though my Master Lamphedon and his Lady bie it deare.
         Ha Lorde Leostines all is loue, that the foole hath confest,
         For I my self did heare all in like case as is exprest.
ostines. Is all true in deede, may I trust thee of thy worde?
ondi.    If you take mee with a lie, thrust me through with your sworde.
eostines. If all be true in deede, and if thou doest not fayne,
         We sure for thy courtesie wee will reward thee with gayne.
         But what is thy name I pray thee confesse?
ondi.    Grauitie noble Lorde, the truth to expresse.

                                                    Grauity

52

Grauetie: thou art welcome to our court, to remaine,
Ya I am the ancienteſt Gentilman ý euer you did entertaine. Condi.

Come on my Lords vn me, with grauitie & the ſole in like caſe, Leoſtine
For wée intend moſt ſecretly to her cloſet dore for to trace.
To ſée if it be true, the which they haue confeſt.

To waight on your honour, wee all are here preſt. Exeunt. All
Ya my good Maſter Lamphedon and Clariſia in like ſort, Condit.
Fortune hath not permitted that longer time you twain ſhuld ſport
would it not gréeue you wiues to ſe your huſbands com from ý ſeas
And cannot haue half a nights lodging but eueri man muſt him diſ·
But diſeaſes or diſeaſe not, if I were in his caſe, (eaſe
At the firſt I would euen to the bed, and vpon her apace.
For it tis my vſe if I be a bed with a woman I take no care,
Untill all the Conſtabels in the towne at my bed ſide are.
Soft, they are comming, alas good louers, you are at a mad ſtaye,
For why, Leoſtines he doth intend to worke your decay.
The beſt is not for me to ſtay their comming into place.
Leaſt I bee taken with a lie which would my doyngs deface.
By your leaue, no more a ſayler will I bee,
But ſtraight will I diſguiſe my ſelf to both parties you ſhall ſée.

¶Here entreth Leoſtines, two Lordes, leadinge
Lamphedon, and Clariſia.

Come Sirs, and bryng away thoſe captiues with ſpéede, Leoſtines
For why, to worke their finall end I fully am decreede.
Ya wretchleſſe dame that thus wouldſt ſéeme for to abuſe thy ſtate
To feede thy filthy fonde deſier, in ſutch a kinde of rate.
Did I immagine day and night thee highly to exalt,
And couldeſt thou ſeeme thus fainedly on bothe ſides for to halt,
Is this thy virgins ſtate, thou wretche, which ſo thou diſt deſiers
Is thy holly ſacred life, which oft thou didſt requier:
Ya careleſſe dame, aſſure thy ſelf without any further pawſe,
Thou ſhalt with this thy louer here according to our lawes
Suſtaine the downe, the which you ment for to beſtow on mee,
That is, for your accurſed crime you bothe ſhall poyſoned bee.
And ý the ſame be ſtraight brought in my lordes I giue you charge
Straight to depart vnto our court & to expreſſe at large
G iij To

To Grauitie, and will him ftraight to depart to our Phiſicion,
And bzyng from thence the ftrongeſt poyſon that is of many a one,
Wherfoze my lozdes incontinent make all the haſt you may.

Poth.   Pour highnes will O noble Lozde your ſeruants ſhall obay   1870

Leoſtines.   Diſpatche my Lozds, foz til they come wée ſhal abide them here.
And caitif well aſſure thy ſelf, thou ſhalt abie this deare.

Lamphe.   O Heauens, how cruelly deale you w̃ vs in changing our eſtate?
How can you ſee the innocent to die in ſutch a rate?
Ha my deare lady, muſt thou ſuſt ine the doome of death foz mee?
Muſt thou foz no offence at all, thzough rankoz poyſoned bee?
Muſt thou O Lady, end thy daies in ſight of me thy freende?
Nay firſt ye mightie powers aboue, vouchſafe my life to ende.
Let not my carefull eyes, alas, in open wiſe remayne,
Untill they ſe her, ha deare gods, thus end her daies thzough paine   1880
O noble lozde, on bended knees her life of thee I craue,
Let me alone ſuſtaine the death which ſrught the ſame to haue.
Haue hir pooze life to end all ſtrife, thy mercie do oſtende,
Seme foz to ſtay, make not away, that which neuer did offend.
Tis I alone, O noble lozde that hath deſerued the death.   (bzeath

Clariſia.   Ha, holde your peace, my louing lozde, in vaine you waſt your
Séeme not to craue thy death alone, my carefull life to ſaue.
Sith thou muſt die, moſt glad am I, the ſelfe ſame death to haue.
O noble lozde Leoſtines, and Maiſter in like caſe,
Uoutchſafe to take ſome pittie here, and graunt to vs ſome grace.   1890
Saue here the life of man and wife, who neuer thought a miſſe.
Towards your ſtate, O wozthy lozde aſſure your ſelf of this.
Although that foole doth séme to faine with that Paraſite alſo,
Séeme not vpon their fozged talke to end our dayes with wo,
But graunt vnto thy ſeruants iuſt, one pardon noble lozde.

Leoſtines.   Leaue of thy ſuite, in vaine thou ſékeſt to haue me to accozde.
But that which you by law deſerue, you ſurely both ſhall haue.
Wherfoze refraine, ſéme not againe of mée the like to craue,
But do pzepare incontinent, and yéld your ſelues to die.

Lamphe.   Then gods voutchſafe foz to réceaue our ſoules to heauens ble.   1900
¶Here entreth Condicions alone with a couered goblet.

Condi.   Ha the Gods pzeſerue your ſtate & ſend your honour long to liue
Pour obedient ſeruant hath bzought here ỹ poyſon which you mind
Unto Lamphedon, and lady Metrea ſhee.   (to giue,

If it please you the Doctor saies tis the strongest ý can deuised bee.
  Geue it me Lamphedon I charge thee to dzinke first the same,  Leostine
  Sith that it is but vayne resistance for to frame :  Lamphe.
Then my deare lady here is to thée in way of our last greetinge
The powers vouchsafe ý in ý heauens we may haue ioyful meting
  Ha my dere lozd, sith néeds thou must, thy loue shal folow straight  Metrea.
  Dispatch I say, make no delay, for long we may not waight.  Leostines
  Ha my deare Lady then here is to thee, though lothsome ý it bee.  Lamphe.
  Taste of the same, for straight ile frame my lozde to follow thee.  Metrea.
  Ha heauens, what lothsom thing is this, ý boileth in my brost?  Lamphe.
Ye powers receaue my spirit I craue, let cozps take his due rest.
Ha my deare parents now a dew & eke eche faithfull freende
Lamphedon héé, with his Lady shéé, their youthful dayes must end.
Farewell ye nobles all, farewell eche Marstall knight,
With whom within my fathers court I often did delight.
And last of all farewel my deare, and faithful Lady true,
Whose heapes of greif I do lament and lothsome state eke rue.
And now farewell with last adue.
  Ha my deare lozde, incontinent I minde thee to persue,  Metrea.
  Well Lady now prepare your selfe of the like sauce to taste.  Leostines.
Séeme not for to lament so longe the time away to waste.
Wherfoze dispatche, take the cup in hand, & dzinke you of the same.
  Wo be to thee Leostines, ý wzongfully hast sought our deaths to  Metrea.
  Wel wel dispatch & make an end for time begins to vade. (frame  Leostines
  Lo Leostines thou shalt not say I go about thee to perswade.  Metrea.
  O stay thy hand, my Metrea deare, and I will saue thy life.  Leostines.
  In faith sir knight you come to late to gaine her as your wife.  Metrea.

## ¶ The Epilogue.

Time is pictured forth to vew all bare and bauld behinde,
  With sickel in his hand to cut when it doth please his minde.
With that his sickell all are cut, and all thing bzought to ende.
As wée are now by Time cut of from farther time to spende.
So time saith to vs seace now here, your audience mutch ye wzong
If farther now to weary them the time ye do pzolonge.
               Wherfoze

Wherfore we render humble thankes for this your courtesse,
And for your quiet patience we thanke you hartely.
Offence we trust we haue none made, but if ought haue scapt a mis
we pardon aske, and will amend when we know what it is. 1940
As duety bindes for our dread Quæne Elizabeth let vs pray,
That god will still defend her grace and bee hir staffe and stay.
Now and alwayes Lord her defend, from foes hir grace lord shield,
And send hir Nestors eares to raine in peace hir realme to wyeld.
Hir counsell Lorde likewise preserue the Preachers in like case,
The Commons eke, the ritch, and pore, Lord send vs all thy grace,

# FINIS.

1949

E ſ [m. ꝑ.) hæc fabula

E ſ, ſ, ſ ὁ ἔωλο hæc fabula præsertim tantis novis rebus: tamen
potuiſe meam lucubrationem nolui